✹125✹
WOOD CLOCK
PATTERNS

JOYCE NOVAK

Sterling Publishing Co., Inc.
New York

To Vicki Lynn Carpenter, my daughter, my pride and joy.

ACKNOWLEDGMENTS

Thank you to Vicki Lynn Carpenter for your encouragement and help with some of the painting. Thanks to my neighbor, Bill Dohrmann, and my son-in-law, Gail Carpenter, for giving me a hand repairing my band saw. Thank you, Kelli and Kevin Andrews, for your expertise and help with the photography. To all my friends, thanks for your interest and encouragement.

Library of Congress Cataloging-in-Publication Data

Novak, Joyce R., 1937–
  125 wood clock patterns / Joyce Novak.
     p. cm.
  Includes index.
  ISBN 1-4027-2261-3
  1. Woodwork—Patterns. 2. Clocks and watches—Design and construction.
I. Title: One hundred twenty-five wood clock patterns. II. Title.
  TT200.N694 2005
  684'.08—dc22

10 9 8 7 6 5 4 3 2 1
Published by Sterling Publishing Co., Inc.
387 Park Avenue South, New York, NY 10016
©2005 by Joyce Novak
This is a revised and expanded version of *101 Wooden Clock Patterns*,
published in 1990 by Sterling Publishing Co., Inc.
Distributed in Canada by Sterling Publishing
℅ Canadian Manda Group, 165 Dufferin Street
Toronto, Ontario, Canada M6K 3H6
Distributed in Great Britain by Chrysalis Books Group PLC
The Chrysalis Building, Bramley Road, London W10 6SP, England
Distributed in Australia by Capricorn Link (Australia) Pty. Ltd.
P.O. Box 704, Windsor, NSW 2756, Australia

Printed in China
All rights reserved.

Sterling ISBN 1-4027-2261-3

For information about custom editions, special sales, premium and corporate
purchases, please contact Sterling Special Sales Department at 800-805-5489 or
specialsales@sterlingpub.com.

CONTENTS

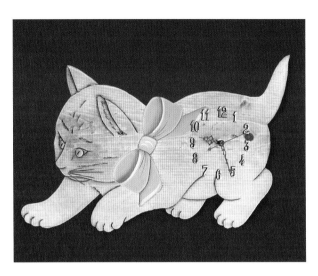

Introduction

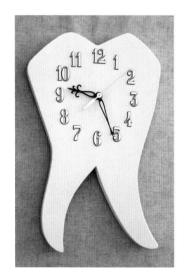

I'm a person who enjoys being busy. I found crafts to be an important part of my world. Crafts filled a void in my life, cheered me when I was lonely, and supplemented my income over the years. I worked for a trucking company for 26 years as a cost accounting clerk. The company went bankrupt in 1984, and, for the first time in my life, I was left without a job. Ten months passed before I found a job that enabled me to support my teenage daughter and myself. During those ten months, I became more involved with the crafts business, going from craft fair to craft fair, and I loved it. (The people were great and I missed them when I quit traveling around the country.) I started by crocheting dolls and découpaging pictures. Then I added clocks to the découpaged pictures. One day at a craft fair, I was asked to make a tooth-shaped clock from wood. I made the tooth clock and the customer ordered four more!

The tooth-shaped clock opened up a whole new world of ideas. Working and creating things from wood had always fascinated me. I began creating patterns and building clocks. At first they were merely stained and varnished silhouettes. Then I began detailing them with a hot tool (wood-burning tool). Shortly after that, I began painting on them. The customers' responses were very rewarding.

My wood shop started with a few inexpensive tools. Gradually I was able to add and upgrade equipment to make the job easier and faster. I was always very busy; eventually I had to give up traveling. I have numerous patterns that my customers asked me to make over and over again. The most popular patterns are in this book. I hope you will enjoy creating these projects as much as I did. They are easy and fun to make. Even the weekend hobbyist with the barest essentials can make any of these clocks, to the pleasure and admiration of family and friends alike. You'll find a wide range of themes in the patterns, including animals suitable for the nursery, western gear for the rec room, and charming patterns for the kitchen or bath. Thanks to quartz clock movements, you need never worry about winding or

setting the clocks. These patterns were originally designed for clocks, but they can easily be converted into many other things, such as banks, weather vanes, coffee mug holders, towel holders, notepad holders, calendar pad holders, coat racks, and necklace holders. Your imagination is the limit. In the Variations section, you will find several of these ideas with patterns drawn out for you.

Instructions for tole painting are included with each pattern.

BASIC INSTRUCTIONS

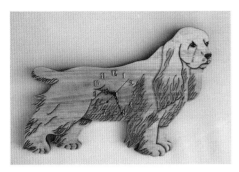

You'll find the patterns in this book versatile and fun to work with. You may use any kind of wood. Most of the items pictured are made with ¾" pine, known as 1" pine (it loses width in finishing). A few items are made with ¾" birch plywood. Some of the clocks are wider than a standard 11¾" pine board. In that case, you may need to match the grain as closely as possible and glue two pieces of pine board together with carpenter's wood glue before cutting. Be sure to let the glue dry thoroughly before working with the lumber (suggested drying time: overnight). If a pattern won't fit on standard 11¾" wide pine, I prefer to either make the pattern a little smaller or to use birch plywood. The birch plywood makes a very nice-looking product. Plywood is also easier to detail with the woodburning tool than pine, especially if you have long, straight lines.

Enlarging Patterns

There are several ways to enlarge a pattern. The easiest and most accurate way is to use a photocopier with variable reduction and enlargement features. The dimensions noted on each pattern serve as suggested sizes to help you get started. Patterns are laid out to fit the pages in the book, and aren't

necessarily lined up to align on the wood grain. In general, once you copy the pattern, try to lay out the pattern so that any narrow parts, such as animal legs, are aligned with the grain of the wood, rather than across it. You will have to enlarge all patterns in the book to get to the sizes listed on the patterns. Let's say a pattern is given at 50% of its actual size. By copying it at the photocopier's 200% enlargement setting, you will end up with the pattern at 100% (50% × 200% = 100%). You may have to photocopy the pattern first at 100%, cut it in quarters, and then photocopy the quarters at the suggested enlargement in order to use the typical office copier to enlarge your pattern. You can also enlarge the patterns without a photocopier using the ½" grid that is part of each pattern, by copying the design square by square onto larger-grid paper, drawing exactly the same number of squares, using any enlargement ratio you desire. If a pattern in this book is approximately 5¾" × 7", and you want your pattern to be 11½" × 14" (twice as large), then draw 1" squares on your final pattern paper (½" × 200% = 1"). You may adjust the size of any pattern to suit your needs or desires. You can also reverse a pattern by "flopping" it, or you can crop a pattern and use just a portion of it. You can also reduce a pattern by copying it smaller, either by the photocopy or grid method.

Another method of copying is to use an inexpensive projector; it can enlarge drawings, patterns, and plans. These machines project

1. Hex nut tighteners.

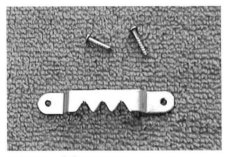

2. Sawtooth hanger.

3. Wood-burning tool.

sharp images onto walls, wood, paper, fabric, etc. Place the original pattern in the glass tray; switch on the projector, focus, and trace. Some projectors enlarge up to 25 times and can project even three-dimensional objects.

Dimensions are given in inches in this book, but if you prefer to work in metric, a metric conversion table (p. 157) will help you convert inches to centimeters.

4. Ultra-thin quartz clock movement.

5. Ornamental clock dial.

6. Numbers for clock faces.

7. Carriage bolts, washers, and wing nuts.

Equipment, Tools, and Supplies

You will need the following tools and supplies:

WOOD TOOLS AND SUPPLIES

- Scroll saw, band saw, or jigsaw
- Hand drill and assorted bits
- Drill press
- ⅜", ½", 2", 2½", and 3" Forstner bits
- Belt sander
- Finish pad sander
- Pliers
- Needle-nose pliers

8. Wood items (top to bottom): 3½" Shaker peg; 3⅜" mug peg; 2⅜" tie peg; ½" screw hole buttons; ⅜" round-top screw hole plugs; wood WELCOME letters; 1" wood hearts; 1" hardwood balls.

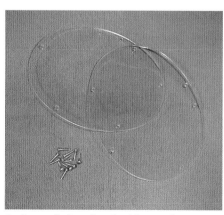

9. Crystal clear bank sides and screws.

- Assorted screwdrivers
- Router and roundover bit
- Hex nut driver
- Hammer
- Sawtooth hangers
- Wood stains
- Wood filler (for plywood edges)
- Wood sealer
- Varnish (for use with acrylic paints)
- Sandpaper (150, 220, 320, 400 grits)
- Wood-burning tool ("hot tool")
- Carpenter's glue
- Tracing paper
- Carbon paper
- Pencil
- Ruler

PAINTING SUPPLIES

- Acrylic craft paints in an assortment of colors; see individual project and painting section for details
- Round brushes (#0 and #2)
- Flat brushes (#2, 4, 6, 8)
- #00 liner brush
- #6 filbert brush
- 2" sponge brush

CLOCK HARDWARE

- Ultra-thin quartz clock movement
- Clock hands
- Adhesive-backed numerals or ready-made multicolor clock dials
- AA batteries for clock

Clock hands are available in several finishes and sizes. The clock hands pictured in the projects have a black or brass finish. The clock kits available have a wide range of clock hand sizes, ranging from 1⁷⁄₁₆" in length to over 4" in length. Remember to choose a set of hour and minute hands that are the appropriate size for the clock face and the wood piece. You don't want to have the hands project beyond the clock itself, nor do you want hands that are so short as to be useless. The second (sweep-second) hand should be approximately the same length as (or slightly shorter than) the minute hand.

Adhesive-backed numerals are also available from clock kit suppliers. They too come in a wide range of sizes, ranging from ⅜" to 1¼" in height. You generally have a choice of Roman or Arabic numerals. You may want to substitute dots or bars for the numerals, or just use numerals at the 12, 3, 6, and 9 o'clock positions, and use the dots or bars to mark the other hours.

Once you have picked your pattern and hardware, you can make the clock by using the step-by-step directions that start on this page.

For nonclock projects, get the other supplies described below, and follow the construction directions given with the project.

SUPPLIES FOR OTHER PROJECTS
Some patterns call for additional parts or supplies, which are listed at the beginning of the instructions for that project. In general, you will need:

For each coat rack:
• Two 1½" screws
• Two ½" wide screw-hole plugs
• Two or three 3½" Shaker pegs

For each notepad or calendar pad holder:
• Two 2" carriage bolts with washers and wing nuts
• 3" × 5" note pad or 10⅝" × 8¼" calendar pad

For each welcome sign:
• Two 1" to 2" lengths of gold- or silver-toned chain
• 4 gold- or silver-toned eye screws

For each bank:
• Two 1½" flat-head screws
• 2 clear plastic 6" × 4½" oval bank sides and screws. You can purchase pre-cut plastic bank sides from some crafts catalogs or stores.

Making a Clock

TRACING, CUTTING, SANDING

Here's how to proceed once you have enlarged and cut out your pattern at the size you want. Trace an outline of the clock pattern onto the wood (Illus. 10). Mark the spot to drill the hole for the clock shaft. Saw the rectangular piece from the wood stock with a jigsaw or other saw. Then saw out the piece, following the line you just traced. Use a scroll saw, band saw, or jigsaw (Illus. 11). In general, you can place the pattern on the wood with the grain going whichever way you wish, except for those patterns that call for the grain to run in a particular direction. These patterns are marked.

Patterns with long, narrow parts (for example, an animal's legs) should be aligned so those parts run with the grain, however. Next, sand the edges, using a grinder/sander or a sanding belt attached to a band saw (Illus. 12), or you may sand the piece by hand (Illus. 13). Note: If you are building the wood piece from birch plywood, you will probably need to fill the holes on the edges with wood filler before sanding. Drill a pilot hole (using an ⅛" bit) from the front, in the spot you marked for the clock shaft (Illus. 14).

Use a Forstner bit to drill a 3" diameter hole approximately ⅜" deep on the back side of the wood piece (Illus. 15). The quartz clock movement will eventually be placed there. Three-inch diameter bits are available for use with a drill press.

10. Tracing the outline and marking the hole for the clock shaft.

11. Sawing out the wood piece.

12. Sanding the edges with a grinder/sander.

13. Sanding the edges by hand.

14. Drilling the pilot hole.

15. Drilling the hole for the quartz clock movement.

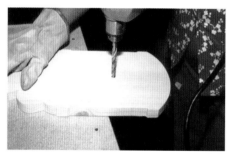

16. Drilling the 5/16" hole for the clock shaft.

17. Sanding the wood piece with medium-grit (220-grit) sandpaper.

18. Taking the sharp edges off the top side of the wood piece.

19. Tracing the detailed pattern onto the wood piece with carbon paper.

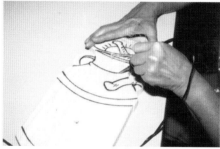

20. Wood-burning the details.

21. Sanding with 320-grit sandpaper after wood-burning.

You needn't drill a circular hole in the wood piece to keep the clock movement in place. As an alternative, you could make your own template to rout out the back of the piece to the exact dimensions of the clock movement. Or you may use a brace and bit. That's what I used until I purchased a drill press. A hole saw and a chisel will work, too. Now that you have a spot for the clock movement, drill a 5/16" hole through the middle of the drilled pilot hole (from the front side) for the clock movement shaft (Illus. 16).

Sand the wood piece thoroughly until it is smooth. Sand both sides using a coarse grade sandpaper, about 150-grit (Illus. 17), then finish with a finer grade sandpaper, 220 or 320-grit. Always sand with the grain of the wood. Any scratch marks will show after varnishing. (Note: Don't use coarse sandpaper if you are building the wood piece from birch plywood. There is only a very thin layer of birch veneer on there, so sand lightly with 220-grit sandpaper instead.) Use 220-grit sandpaper to take the sharp edges off the top side of the wood piece next (Illus. 18).

WOOD-BURNING

Trace the enlarged, detailed pattern lightly onto the wood piece by placing any type of carbon paper face down between the pattern and the wood piece (Illus. 19). Trace over all the lines with a pencil or stylus. Remove pattern and carbon paper. Next, carefully follow all the traced lines with the wood-burning tool to detail (Illus. 20). If you have never used the wood-burning tool before, practice first on a scrap piece of lumber to get a feel for the tool. Wood-burning is fun and easy.

Anyone can learn to do it. After the wood piece is wood-burned and detailed, sand it again with 220 or 320-grit sandpaper to remove pencil marks, ashes, and sap (Illus. 21).

SAFETY

Here are a few important guidelines to make sure you work safely. When using power machinery, be alert. The band saw blade teeth should point downward toward the table; make sure blade tension and blade tracking are both properly adjusted; keep hands and fingers away from the blade; make escape cuts; and turn the machine off before removing scrap pieces from the table near the blade. Whether sawing or sanding, don't wear jewelry or loose clothing; tie back long hair; hold the wood firmly; wear a face shield or safety glasses; wear dust and filter masks, especially when sanding; and keep your machine and work area as clean as possible. Read the manufacturer's labels and warnings before using any power tools. Be sure no small children have access to your work area. Store any flammable materials in a fireproof cabinet if possible. Stain and seal in a well-ventilated area.

The wood-burning tool should be handled with care. Never place it near flammable material (rags, sawdust, paper). Unplug the tool when you're finished with it; don't leave it on when you're doing something else. Place the hot end on some type of stand or fire-resistant surface when you put it down for a moment. As with all electrical appliances, make sure the tool is in a grounded socket, and avoid shocks. Read the manufacturer's label and warnings before you use the tool.

STAINING AND SEALING

Stains take differently on different woods. Before staining the detailed wood piece, test the color on scrap lumber. Most of the clocks and variations pictured are stained with American walnut (by Minwax). Using a soft cloth, stain both sides of the wood piece to your liking (Illus. 22). Let the stain dry thoroughly, approximately 8 to 12 hours.

Next, seal the wood piece on both sides with an all-purpose sealer. Follow the directions of the sealer product you are using. Now you may varnish using a good quality brush or spray with a clear gloss finish following the directions of the product you are using. Or proceed by following the painting directions as outlined in this book after you have applied the sealer. Varnish or spray after painting.

Find the center of balance by dangling the piece in front of you, holding it between your thumb and index finger. Nail a sawtooth hanger to that center spot on the back of the wood piece (Illus. 23).

INSERTING THE CLOCK MECHANISM AND NUMERALS

Put a rubber gasket on the shaft of the clock movement and insert it through the ⁵⁄₁₆" hole (Illus. 24). Then fasten it, using the washer and the hex nut provided with the clock movement kit (Illus. 25). Tighten both until the movement is snug, but don't overtighten them. The template given on page 155 will allow you to place all 12 numerals on the clock face accurately and to create clock faces of varying diameters.

The diameter of the clock face depends upon the size of the finished wood piece. Choose numerals that fit the clock face. Copy and cut

22. Staining the wood piece using a soft cloth. Remember to let the stain dry thoroughly, usually about 8 to 12 hours.

23. Nailing the sawtooth hanger on the center of balance.

24. Inserting the quartz clock movement. The clock shaft should fit through the ⁵⁄₁₆" hole.

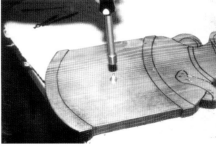

25. Tightening the washer and the hex nut.

26. The template is used to position the numbers on the clock face.

27. Putting the three clock hands in place.

28. The completed clock without tole painting (left) and with tole painting (right).

the clock face template to the desired size for the clock dial. Hang the clock on the wall; adjust the template to be sure the face will be straight; then apply the adhesive-backed numerals. Place each numeral at an intersection of a radiating spoke and the circle (Illus. 26).

Using the minute hand, turn the clock movement shaft to 12 (the slot on the minute hand and the slot on the shaft should line up); then remove the minute hand and slide the hour hand onto the shaft, pointing it to 9. The hour hand fits rather tightly on the shaft, but keep working it down until it almost touches the threaded part of the shaft. Now put the minute hand on, pointing it to 12 (which you just preset), and then put on the tiny nut. Tighten the

nut with needle-nose pliers. Press the second (sweep-second) hand on top of the minute hand (Illus. 27). The second hand will slip into the small hole in the clock movement shaft. Mini-quartz clock movements are excellent and accurate time-keepers. Insert one AA battery and set the time. The clock is now complete (Illus. 28).

If you decide to use the multi-color clock dial component, you will need to rout the 3" hole for the clock movement ½" deep instead of ⅜" deep. This allows the clock movement shaft to extend an extra ⅛" through the front of the clock. The clock hands will then clear the multicolor clock face component.

Painting

Instead of the basic finish we previously described (stain, seal, and varnish), you may want to finish the wood piece by giving it more character and life with painting. You will need a good selection of acrylic craft paints in various colors, a liner brush (#00), several flat brushes, round brushes (#0 and #2), filbert brush (#6), and a 2" sponge brush. See the materials list earlier in this chapter for a full list of painting supplies. The colors I used to paint these clocks and variations were Ceramcoat Acrylic Paints by Delta and Jo Sonja's Rich Gold and Silver, but you can use any acrylic paints and mix your own colors if you choose. We have included a color chart so you can easily see the colors described in the clock painting instructions and, if necessary, substitute another brand of colors or mix your own.

Each of the wooden clock patterns and pattern variations in this book includes painting instructions and a photo to guide you. Here in the basic painting section there are several illustrations to show you the different painting strokes and how to paint the eyes, ears, borders, flowers, leaves, bows, fringe, and lace, and how to shadow, highlight, and dry-brush. Before you paint, use the wood-burning tool to outline the areas to be painted.

STROKES

Here are some examples of painting strokes you'll need to use, and some helpful notes (Illus. 1).

Comma stroke. Use a round brush.
Upside-down comma stroke. Use a round brush.
Teardrop stroke. Use a round brush. Basically the same as a comma, except it is straight.
Float. Using a flat brush, load one side.
C-stroke. Use a flat brush.
Double-load. Load the flat brush with two different colors, one color on one side and another color on the other side.
Triple-load. Using a flat brush, load it with (for example) blue spruce. Then load one side with coral and the other side with silver.
Shadow and highlight. Shadow and highlight using the float stroke. Shadow with the dark color on the under side; highlight with the light color on the top.
Dry-brush. Detail with the wood-burning tool. Dip an old, frayed brush in paint and wipe off the excess on scrap paper; then pull strokes through mane and tail (for example). Next, with the liner brush, pull a darker color through the lines.

EYES

Here are some typical eyes and how to make them (Illus. 2). You'll see these on many of the animal photos.

Eye 1. Wood-burn the outline of the eye; then paint the iris black. Paint a white upside-down comma on one side and a tiny white comma on the other.
Eye 2. Wood-burn a circle. Paint it white. Paint the smaller portion black. Place a white dot in the center of the black.

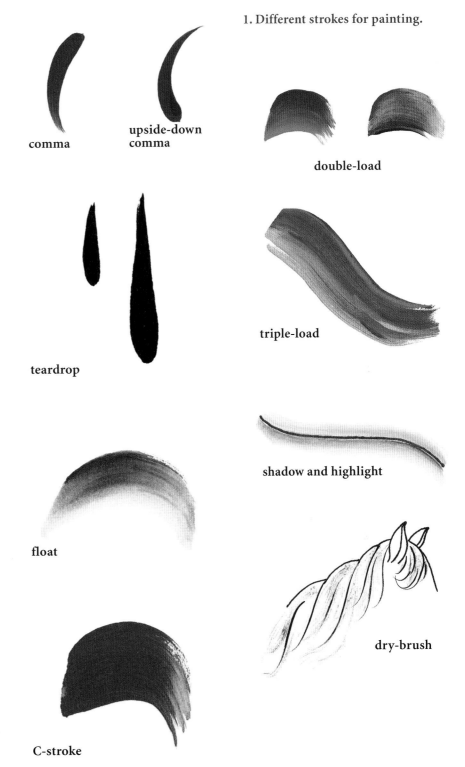

comma

upside-down comma

double-load

teardrop

triple-load

float

shadow and highlight

C-stroke

dry-brush

Eye 3. Wood-burn the outline of the eye. Paint the eye black. Paint an upside-down white comma on one side and a tiny white comma on the other. Paint black eyelashes. Float adobe on the cheek and paint a tiny white comma under the eye on the adobe.
Eye 4. Wood-burn the outline of the eye. Paint the eye black. Paint a white upside-down comma on one side and a tiny white comma on the other side. Paint black eyelashes.

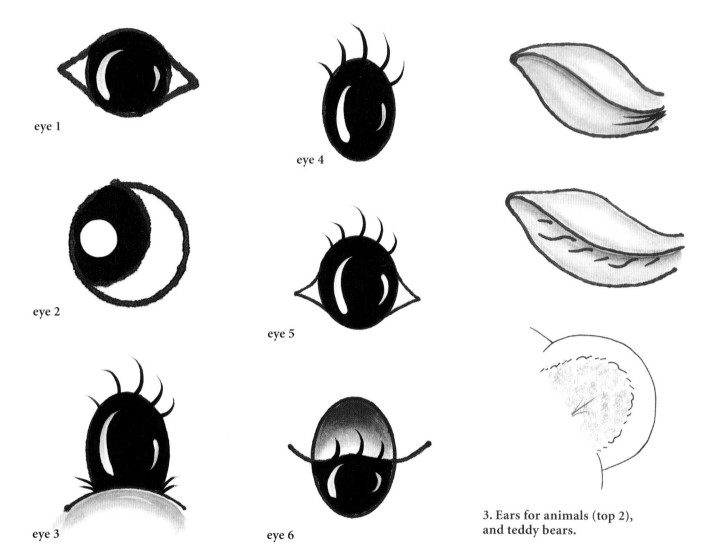

eye 1

eye 2

eye 3

eye 4

eye 5

eye 6

3. Ears for animals (top 2), and teddy bears.

2. Eyes

Eye 5. Wood-burn the outline of the eye. Paint the eyeball black. Paint an upside-down white comma on one side and a smaller white comma on the other side. Paint black eyelashes.

Eye 6. Wood-burn the outline of the eye. Paint the eyeball black with a white upside-down comma on one side and a tiny white comma on the other. Float brown velvet on the eyelid. Paint black eyelashes.

EARS

Ears for animals. Detail ears with the wood-burning tool. Use the shadow-and-highlight technique. Paint little black hairs on the inside (Illus. 3).

Teddy bear ears. Detail with the wood-burning tool. With a frayed brush, daub maple sugar tan in the center of the ear. Then pull lines with a liner brush and adobe paint (Illus. 3).

FLOWERS AND LEAVES

Flowers 1. Take a flat paintbrush, double-load with white and whatever color of flower you want, and do a C-stroke for the upper side. Then do a C-stroke starting at the same point, going in the opposite direction, for the bottom of the flower. Put tiny dots in the center. Pull lines for green stems and use comma strokes for leaves. Put a green dot where the stem and flower meet (Illus. 4).

Flowers 2. Using the flower color, make five dots in a circle. Then put a dot of another color in the center. Pull lines with green for stems and make comma strokes for leaves (Illus. 4).

Leaves. Using a #6 filbert brush, double-load with dark jungle green and Seminole green. Go in one direction for one side and,

4. Flowers 1 (top) and Flowers 2 (bottom).

7. Fringe.

8. Lace.

5. Leaves.

6. Two styles of bow, bow 1 (top) and bow 2 (bottom).

9. Comma-and-dot border.

starting at the same spot, go in the other direction for the other side; finish off with a twist of the brush at the leaf tip (Illus. 5).

BOWS, FRINGE, LACE, BORDER
Bow 1 and Bow 2. Wood-burn the outside lines of the bow and the knot. These bows are painted Wedgwood blue. To detail, side-load a flat brush with Cape Cod blue for shadowing. Side-load with blue mist to highlight. With a liner brush, pull lines from the knot out toward each side of the bow. Then paint gold comma strokes on the ends of the ribbon and tiny gold commas on the knot (Illus. 6).
Fringe. Using the wood end of a brush, make dots around the item on which you want fringes. Let dots dry; then, with a liner brush, pull lines for fringe (Illus. 7).
Lace. Double-load a flat brush with a light color and a dark color (I used heritage blue and blue mist here). Make C-strokes around the item on which you want lace. Then pull lines with the dark color to make the fabric look gathered. Paint gold commas around the edge. Use the wood ends of brushes to make different sizes of dots. Use a stylus to make tiny dots (Illus. 8).
Comma-and-dot border. Make comma strokes and dots, using colors of the item you are painting (Illus. 9).

Color Chart

Color chart for tole painting colors, using Ceramcoat acrylic paints from Delta. Use as reference guide for painting. You can use other brands, matching the colors shown here. Silver and gold are from Jo Sonja.

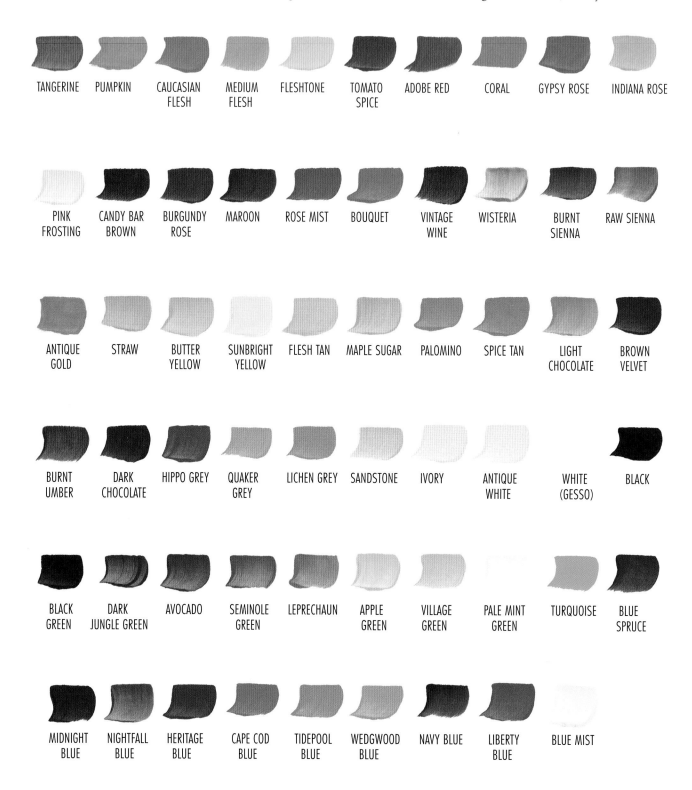

TANGERINE PUMPKIN CAUCASIAN FLESH MEDIUM FLESH FLESHTONE TOMATO SPICE ADOBE RED CORAL GYPSY ROSE INDIANA ROSE

PINK FROSTING CANDY BAR BROWN BURGUNDY ROSE MAROON ROSE MIST BOUQUET VINTAGE WINE WISTERIA BURNT SIENNA RAW SIENNA

ANTIQUE GOLD STRAW BUTTER YELLOW SUNBRIGHT YELLOW FLESH TAN MAPLE SUGAR PALOMINO SPICE TAN LIGHT CHOCOLATE BROWN VELVET

BURNT UMBER DARK CHOCOLATE HIPPO GREY QUAKER GREY LICHEN GREY SANDSTONE IVORY ANTIQUE WHITE WHITE (GESSO) BLACK

BLACK GREEN DARK JUNGLE GREEN AVOCADO SEMINOLE GREEN LEPRECHAUN APPLE GREEN VILLAGE GREEN PALE MINT GREEN TURQUOISE BLUE SPRUCE

MIDNIGHT BLUE NIGHTFALL BLUE HERITAGE BLUE CAPE COD BLUE TIDEPOOL BLUE WEDGWOOD BLUE NAVY BLUE LIBERTY BLUE BLUE MIST

SILVER RICH GOLD

Walking Horse Clock

5/16" hole for clock shaft

Painting and Finishing

1. Stain and seal whole surface. Shadow with brown velvet and highlight with palomino tan.
2. Paint eyes, mane, tail, and hooves black. Paint tiny white commas on eyes.
3. Highlight mane, tail, and hooves with lichen grey. Paint halter candy bar brown. Highlight with Indiana rose. Put gold dots on halter.
4. Spray with a clear high-gloss acrylic finish.
5. Attach a sawtooth hanger on back. Assemble clock movement, numbers, and hands on the finished piece.

Copy pattern at 260%. Finished size: about 11½" wide by 15¼" high.

Covered Wagon Clock

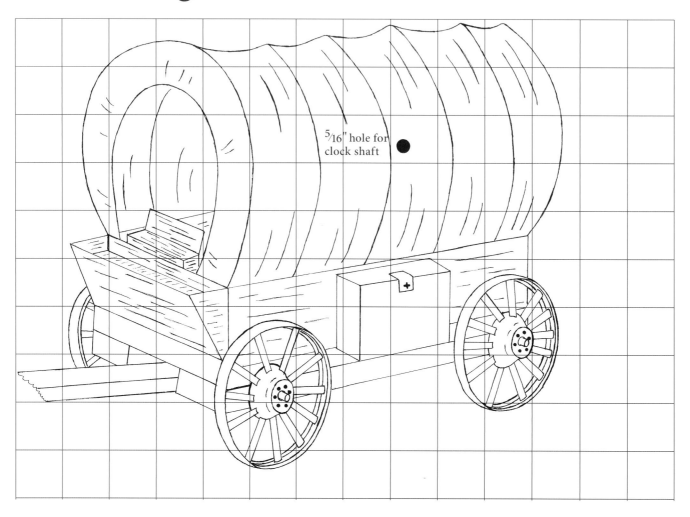

5/16" hole for clock shaft

Painting and Finishing

1. Stain and seal whole surface.
2. Shadow with brown velvet. Highlight with palomino tan.
3. Put a brown velvet wash on spokes and drums of wheels, seat, tongue, and toolbox. Highlight with palomino tan. Paint axles and rim of wheels black. Highlight with lichen grey.
4. Put a palomino tan wash on inside of wagon cover. Paint cover antique white. Shadow with flesh tan and highlight with white.
5. Spray with a clear high-gloss acrylic finish.
6. Attach a sawtooth hanger on back. Assemble clock movement, numbers, and hands on the finished piece.

Copy pattern at 230%. Finished size: about 13¼" wide by 10¼" high.

Horses and Chariot Clock

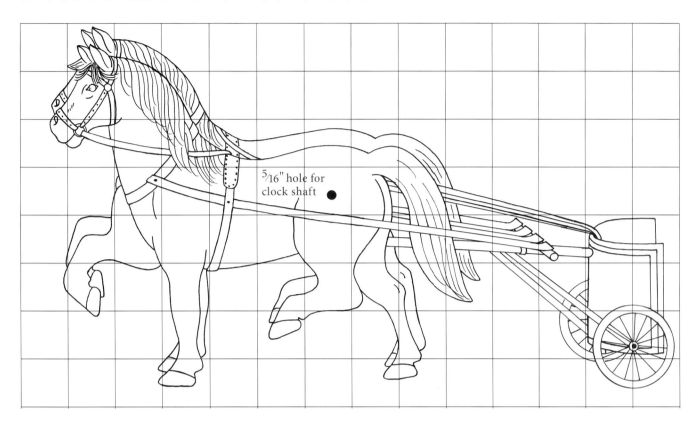

5/16" hole for clock shaft

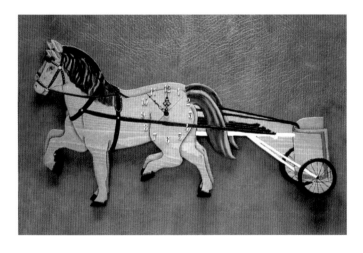

Painting and Finishing

1. Stain and seal whole surface.
2. Shadow with brown velvet. Highlight with palomino tan.
3. Double-load flat brush with black and palomino tan to paint manes and tails. Paint eye, hooves, and wheels black. Highlight with lichen grey. Paint a tiny white comma on eye.
4. Paint bridles and harness brown velvet. Highlight with palomino tan. Put gold dots on bridles and harness.
5. Paint rods and tongue on chariot lichen grey. Highlight with white. Paint a red trim on the chariot.
6. Spray with a clear high-gloss acrylic finish.
7. Attach a sawtooth hanger on back. Assemble clock movement, numbers, and hands on the finished piece.

Copy pattern at 315%. Finished size: about 20½" wide by 12" tall.

Saddle Horse Clock

⁵⁄₁₆" hole for clock shaft

Painting and Finishing

1. Stain and seal whole surface.
2. Shadow with brown velvet and highlight with palomino tan.
3. Paint eye and hooves black. Paint tiny white comma on eye. Highlight hooves with lichen grey.
4. Paint saddle spice tan. Shadow with burnt umber. Highlight with ivory.
5. Paint the spaces between front legs, between the reins, and between the reins and the neck and head, as well as the space between the tail and back leg, black.
6. Dry-brush with burnt umber through mane and tail; then pull black lines through same.
7. Paint decorative straps around horn and stirrup burnt umber. Highlight with palomino tan.
8. Paint the blanket and bridle candy bar brown. Highlight with Indiana rose.
9. Paint ring around straps, horn, and hardware on bridle gold. Put gold dots on bridle and saddle. Paint tiny gold commas around edge of blanket.

10. Spray with a clear high-gloss acrylic finish.
11. Attach a sawtooth hanger on back. Assemble clock movement, numbers, and hands on the finished piece.

Copy pattern at 260%. Finished size: about 13" wide by 13" tall.

Saddle Clock

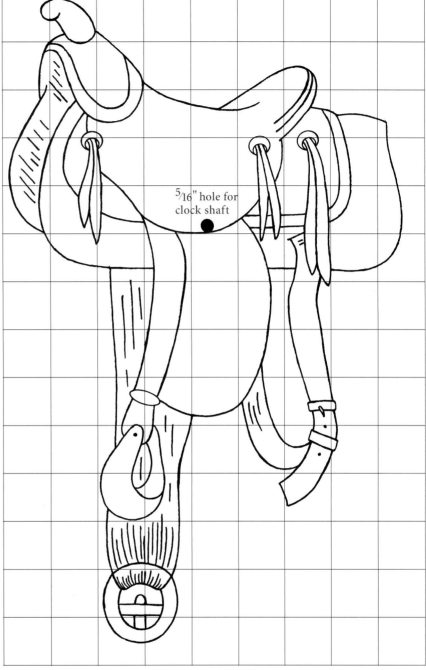

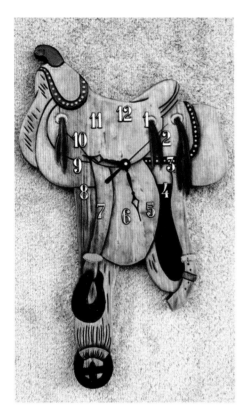

Painting and Finishing

1. Stain and seal whole surface.

2. Shadow with brown velvet. Highlight with palomino tan.

3. Put a brown velvet wash on the inside of the saddle (left side). Paint black on the horn, stirrup, cinch buckle, trim on saddle, and the space inside the strap. Highlight with lichen grey.

4. Paint the decorative straps candy bar brown. Highlight with Indiana rose. Paint gold on the buckle of the large strap, hardware above stirrup, and the rings around the top of the decorative straps. Put gold dots around the horn and on the black trim.

5. Spray with a clear high-gloss acrylic finish.

6. Attach a sawtooth hanger on back. Assemble clock movement, numbers, and hands on the finished piece.

Copy pattern at 235%. Finished size: about 10" wide by 15¾" tall.

Hat and Spur Clock

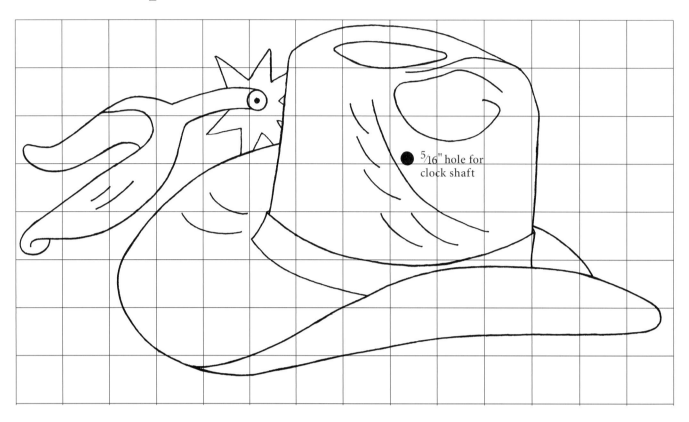

5⁄16" hole for clock shaft

Painting and Finishing

1. Stain and seal whole surface.
2. Shadow with brown velvet. Highlight with palomino tan.
3. Paint band on hat black and highlight with lichen grey.
4. Paint spur lichen grey. Shadow with hippo grey and highlight with white.
5. Spray with a clear high-gloss acrylic finish.
6. Attach a sawtooth hanger on back. Assemble clock movement, numbers, and hands on the finished piece.

Copy pattern at 220%. Finished size: about 15⅛" wide by 8" high.

Cowboy Boots Clock

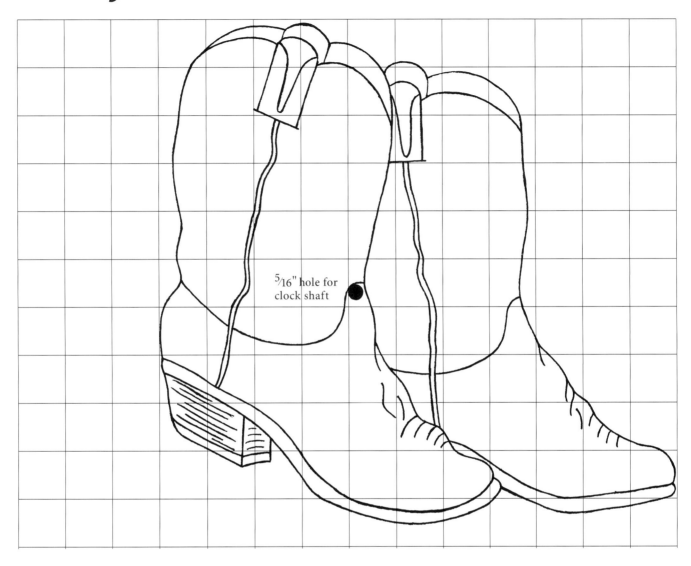

5/16" hole for clock shaft

Painting and Finishing

1. Stain and seal whole surface.
2. Shadow with brown velvet. Highlight with palomino tan.
3. Paint soles and outside section of pull tabs black. Highlight with lichen grey.
4. Paint strip down the side of the boots, and inside and back side of pull tabs candy bar brown. Highlight with Indiana rose.
5. Spray with a clear high-gloss acrylic finish.
6. Attach a sawtooth hanger on back. Assemble clock movement, numbers, and hands on the finished piece.

Copy pattern at 200%. Finished size: about 11" wide by 10½" tall.

Pistol Clock

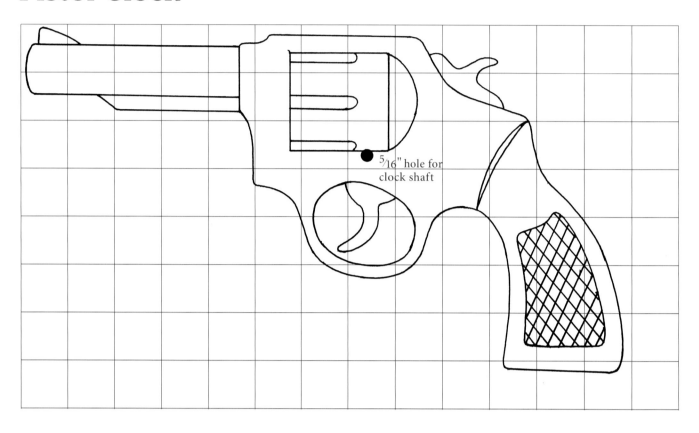

5/16" hole for clock shaft

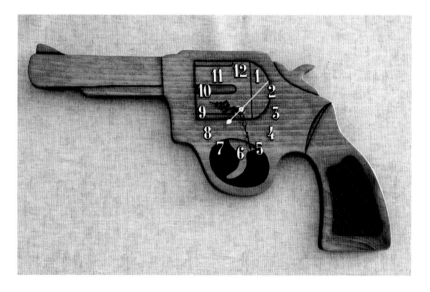

Painting and Finishing

1. Stain and seal whole surface.
2. Shadow with brown velvet and highlight with palomino tan.
3. Paint the decorative section on the handle brown velvet. Paint black in the space around the trigger.
4. Spray with a clear high-gloss acrylic finish.
5. Attach a sawtooth hanger on back. Assemble clock movement, numbers, and hands on the finished piece.

Copy pattern at 250%. Finished size: about 16" wide by 9" high.

Horse at Gate Clock or Welcome

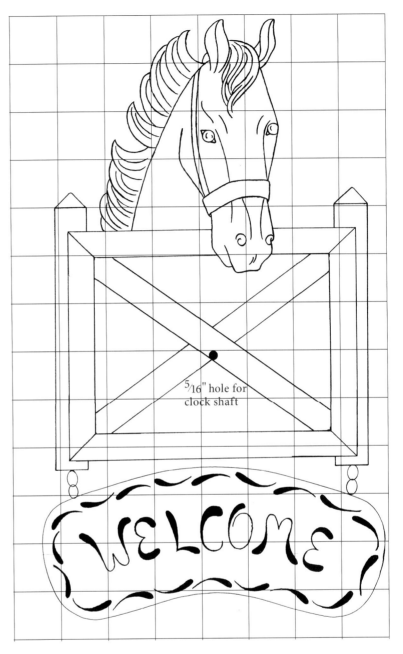

Clock

The clock pictured is made from ¾" birch plywood, stained with American walnut.

1. Mark the spot for the clock shaft and drill a pilot hole with ⅛" bit. Using a Forstner bit, drill a 3" diameter hole approximately ⅜" deep on the back side of the wood piece. From the front side, drill a ⁵⁄₁₆" hole through the middle of the drilled pilot hole for the clock movement shaft.
2. Stain and seal the whole surface.
3. Shadow with brown velvet and highlight with palomino tan.
4. Paint eyes and mane black. Highlight the mane with lichen grey. Paint tiny white commas on the eyes.
5. Paint the halter candy bar brown. Highlight with Indiana rose. Put gold dots on the halter.
6. Put a burnt umber wash on the frame and cross pieces of the gate.
7. Spray with a clear high-gloss acrylic finish.

8. Drill a tiny hole in upper right corner of gate, and hang a 5½" chain around post, attached at both ends to an eye screw in the hole.
9. Attach a sawtooth hanger on back. Assemble clock movement, numbers, and hands on the finished piece.

Copy pattern at 290% for clock. Finished size: about 9⅞" wide by 14" tall.

⁵⁄₁₆" hole for clock shaft

Horse Welcome Sign

Additional supplies for welcome sign:

- Two 1" lengths of gold or silver-toned chain
- One 5½" length of gold or silver-toned chain
- One 19" length of gold or silver-toned chain
- Five gold or silver-toned eye screws

1. Trace outline of each pattern (horse and welcome board) on poster paper, cut out, and trace on ¾" pine wood.
2. Saw out and sand well.
3. Trace detailed pattern onto the horse wood piece and detail with a wood-burning tool. Sand again with 320 grit sandpaper to remove trace marks, sap, and ashes.
4. Stain and seal whole surface.
5. Shadow with brown velvet and highlight with palomino tan.
6. Paint eyes and mane black. Highlight the mane with lichen grey. Paint tiny white commas on the eyes.
7. Paint the halter candy bar brown. Highlight with Indiana rose. Put gold dots on the halter. Put a burnt umber wash on the frame and cross pieces of the gate.
8. Paint "WELCOME" on the sign board with black. Paint candy bar brown commas and gold dots around edge. Use wood end of brush to make the dots.
9. Spray with a clear high-gloss acrylic finish.
10. Drill tiny holes in posts (at both top and bottom), in gate, and in welcome board for eye screws (see photo). Attach a 19" length chain to post tops for the hanger. Put an eye screw in the upper right corner of the gate and attach both ends of a 5½" chain to it. Swing chain around post. Assemble the welcome sign using four eye screws and two 1" lengths of chain to connect the sign to the gate.

Copy pattern on page 23 at 270% for welcome sign. Approximate finished size of horse at gate with welcome sign attached is 9⅞" wide by 18¼" high.

Walking Kitten with Bow Clock

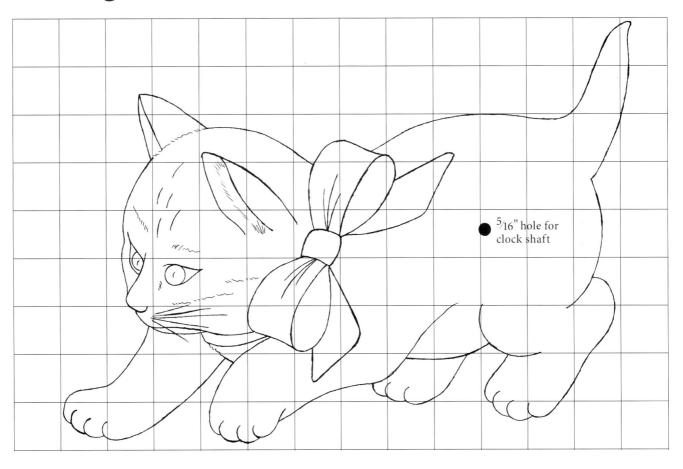

5/16" hole for clock shaft

Painting and Finishing

1. Stain and seal whole surface. Shadow with brown velvet. Highlight with palomino tan.
2. Paint the eyes Wedgwood blue. Shadow with Cape Cod blue and highlight with blue mist. Paint a tiny upside-down teardrop stroke with midnight blue in the center of each eye.
3. Paint the ribbon Cape Cod blue and shadow with midnight blue. Highlight with blue mist.
4. Paint gold comma strokes on ends of the ribbon and around the edge. Put tiny gold commas on the knot.
5. Spray with a clear high-gloss acrylic finish.
6. Attach a sawtooth hanger on back. Assemble clock movement, numbers, and hands on the finished piece.

Copy pattern at 185%. Finished size: about 14½" wide by 11¼" tall.

Seated Kitten Clock

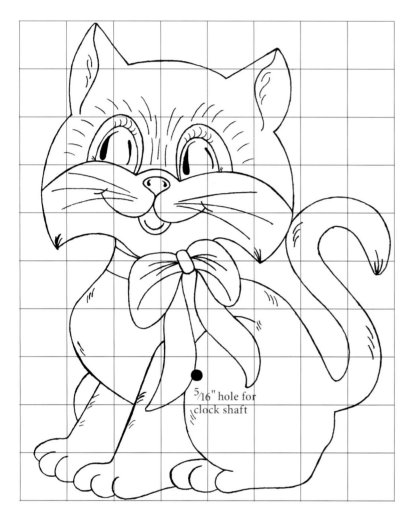

5/16" hole for clock shaft

Painting and Finishing

1. Stain and seal whole surface.
2. Shadow with brown velvet. Highlight with palomino tan.
3. Paint eyes, nose, and space between body and tail black. Paint white upside-down comma on the left side of the eyes and a tiny white comma on the other side. Paint tiny upside-down commas on the nose for nostrils. Float adobe on the tongue and highlight with tiny white comma. Paint black eyelashes.
4. Paint the bow heritage blue. Shadow with midnight blue and highlight with Wedgwood blue. Paint a gold comma on each end of the ribbon and tiny comma on the knot.
5. Spray with a clear high-gloss acrylic finish.
6. Attach a sawtooth hanger on back. Assemble clock movement, numbers, and hands on the finished piece.

Copy pattern at 235%. Finished size: about 9¼" wide by 12½" tall.

Puppy with Ball Clock

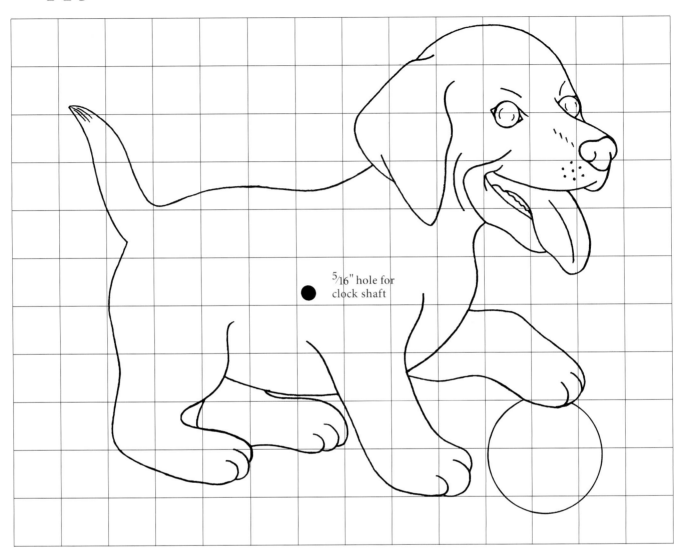

5/16" hole for clock shaft

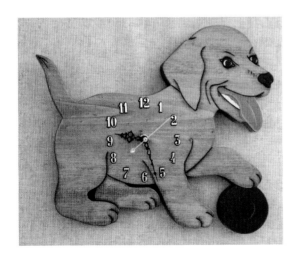

Painting and Finishing

1. Stain and seal whole surface. Shadow with brown velvet and highlight with palomino tan.
2. Paint eyes and nose black. Highlight nose with lichen grey. Paint an upside-down white comma on the left side of each eye and a tiny comma on the other side.
3. Paint the tongue coral. Shadow with adobe and highlight with antique white.
4. Paint the teeth antique white and highlight with white.
5. Paint the ball tomato spice. Highlight with Indiana rose.
6. Spray with a clear high-gloss acrylic finish.
7. Attach a sawtooth hanger on back. Assemble clock movement, numbers, and hands on the finished piece.

Copy pattern at 200%. Finished size: about 11¾" wide by 10¼" tall.

Bulldog Clock

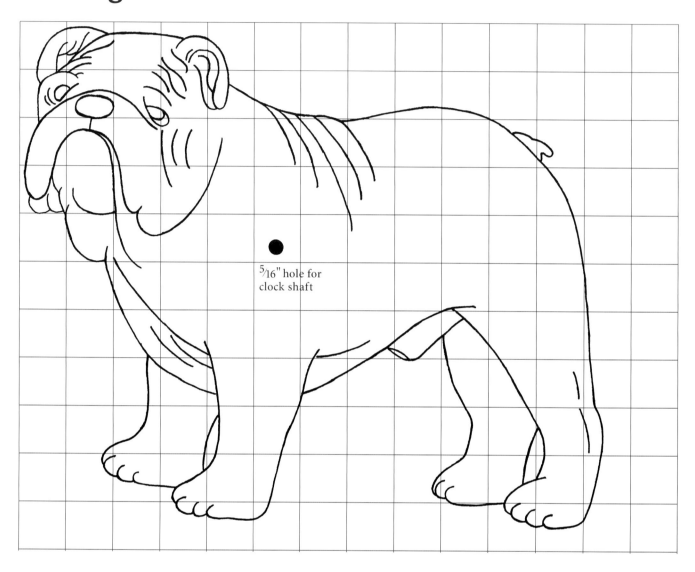

⁵⁄₁₆" hole for
clock shaft

Painting and Finishing

1. Stain and seal whole surface. Shadow with brown velvet and highlight with palomino tan.
2. Paint eyes, nose, and spaces between legs black. Highlight nose with lichen grey. Paint upside-down commas on the nose for the nostrils with lichen grey. Paint tiny white commas on the eyes.
3. Spray with a clear high-gloss acrylic finish.
4. Attach a sawtooth hanger on back. Assemble clock movement, numbers, and hands on the finished piece.

Copy pattern at 200%. Finished size: about 12½" wide by 10½" tall.

German Shepherd Clock

Painting and Finishing

1. Stain and seal whole surface. Shadow with brown velvet and highlight with palomino tan.
2. Paint eye and nose black. Highlight nose with lichen grey. Paint an upside-down lichen grey comma on the nose for the nostril. Paint tiny white commas on eye.
3. Paint the tongue coral. Shadow with adobe and highlight with antique white.
4. Paint the teeth antique white and highlight with white.
5. Spray with a clear high-gloss acrylic finish.
6. Attach a sawtooth hanger on back. Assemble clock movement, numbers, and hands on the finished piece.

Copy pattern at 200%. Finished size: about 8½" wide by 9½" tall.

5/16" hole for clock shaft

Cocker Spaniel Clock

5/16" hole for clock shaft

Painting and Finishing

1. Stain and seal whole surface. Shadow with brown velvet and highlight with palomino tan.
2. Paint eyes and nose black. Highlight nose with lichen grey. Paint tiny white commas on each eye.
3. Spray with a clear high-gloss acrylic finish.
4. Attach a sawtooth hanger on back. Assemble clock movement, numbers, and hands on the finished piece.

Copy pattern at 230%. Finished size: about 16" wide by 11" tall.

Poodle Clock

Painting and Finishing

1. Stain and seal whole surface. Shadow with brown velvet and highlight with palomino tan.
2. Paint eyes and nose black. Paint white comma on the left side of each eye and a tiny comma on the right side. Paint small upside-down white commas on each side of the nose for nostrils.
3. Paint the tongue coral and highlight with white.
4. Paint the bow and collar Wedgwood blue. Shadow with Cape Cod blue and highlight with blue mist.
5. Paint a tiny gold comma on the ends of the ribbon and on the knot.
6. Spray with a clear high-gloss acrylic finish.
7. Attach a sawtooth hanger on back. Assemble clock movement, numbers, and hands on the finished piece.

Copy pattern at 230%. Finished size: about 10½" wide by 14" tall.

5/16" hole for clock shaft

Tiger Clock

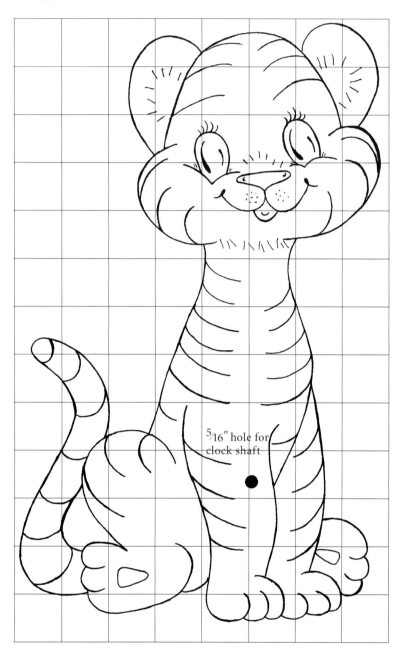

5/16" hole for clock shaft

Painting and Finishing

1. Stain and seal whole surface. Shadow with brown velvet. Highlight with palomino tan.
2. Paint eyes, nose, pads on his feet, and the space between tail and back leg black. Paint an upside-down white comma on the left side of each eye and a tiny comma on the other side. Paint tiny upside-down white commas on the nose for nostrils. Paint black eyelashes.
3. Dip an old frayed brush into brown velvet and remove excess, then lightly daub on inside of ears. Float adobe on the tongue and highlight with a tiny white comma.
4. Spray with a clear high-gloss acrylic finish.
5. Attach a sawtooth hanger on back. Assemble clock movement, numbers, and hands on the finished piece.

Copy pattern at 220%. Finished size: about 8½" wide by 13¾" tall.

Elephant Clock

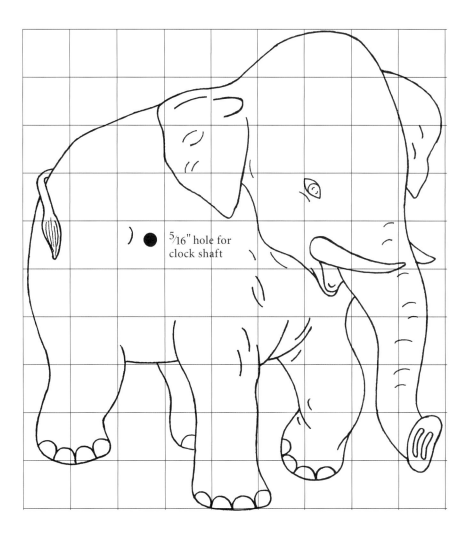

${}^{5}/_{16}$" hole for clock shaft

Painting and Finishing

1. Stain and seal whole surface. Shadow with brown velvet. Highlight with palomino tan.
2. Paint tusks antique white. Shadow with antique gold. Highlight with white.
3. Paint eye and toes black. Highlight toes with lichen grey. Put tiny white commas on eye.
4. Spray with a clear high-gloss acrylic finish.
5. Attach a sawtooth hanger on back. Assemble clock movement, numbers, and hands on the finished piece.

Copy pattern at 215%. Finished size: about 9¾" wide by 11" high.

Butterfly Clock

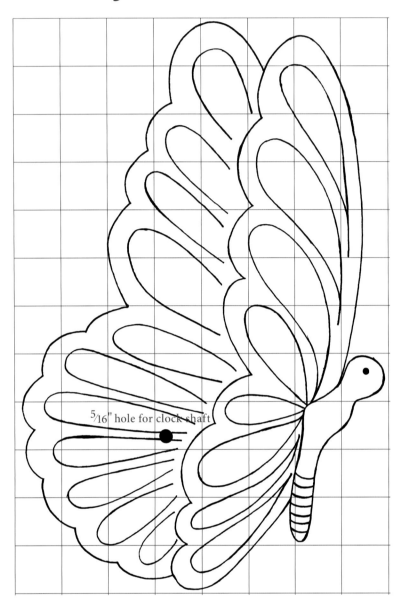

5/16" hole for clock shaft

Additional supplies for this project: Two 6" lengths of brass wire for the antennae

Painting and Finishing

1. Stain and seal whole surface. Shadow with brown velvet and highlight with palomino tan.
2. Paint the loop shapes on the lower wings yellow. Shadow with straw and highlight with antique white.
3. Paint the loop shapes on the upper wings pumpkin. Shadow with tangerine and highlight with antique white. With the wood end of your brush, make black dots around the edge of the wings.
4. Float brown velvet on the lower part of the butterfly body (tail). Put a black dot for the eye.

5. Drill two tiny holes in the top of the head, side by side, for the antennas (two 6" lengths of brass wire). With needle-nose pliers, turn one end of each wire in a small circle.
6. Insert the straight ends of the wire antennae in the holes on the top of the head.
7. Spray with a clear high-gloss acrylic finish.
8. Attach a sawtooth hanger to the back. Assemble clock movement, numbers, and hands on the finished piece.

Copy pattern at 220%. Finished size: about 8½" wide by 13" high.

Turtle Clock

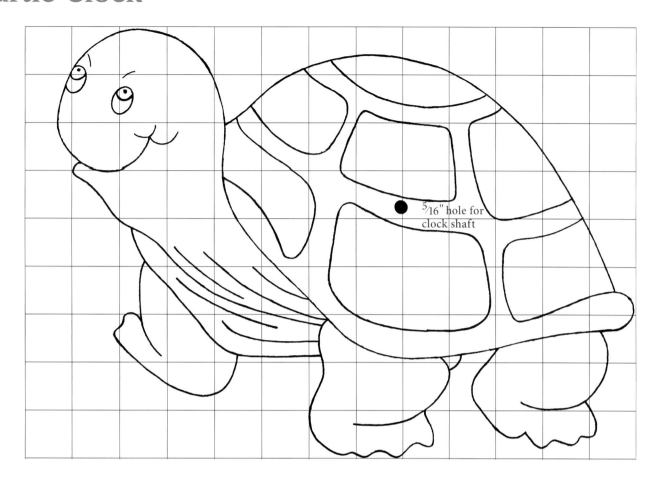

5/16" hole for clock shaft

Painting and Finishing

1. Stain and seal whole surface. Shadow with brown velvet. Highlight with palomino tan.
2. Paint lower part of eyes black and the upper part white with a black dot in the center of the white. Paint black brows with commas.
3. Paint the big areas on the shell avocado green (see photo).
4. Spray with a clear high-gloss acrylic finish.
5. Attach a sawtooth hanger on back. Assemble clock movement, numbers, and hands on the finished piece.

Copy pattern at 220%. Finished size: about 13½" wide by 10" tall.

White-Tailed Deer Clock

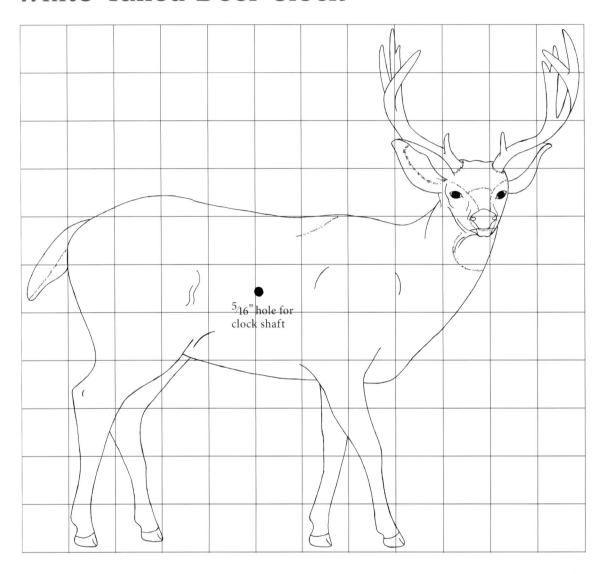

$5/16$" hole for
clock shaft

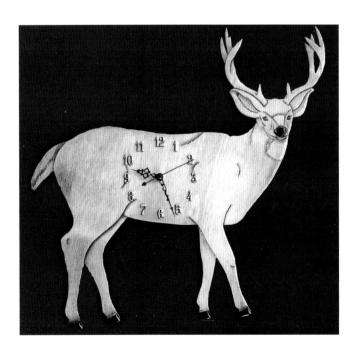

Painting and Finishing

1. Stain and seal whole surface. Shadow with brown velvet and highlight with palomino tan.
2. Paint eyes, nose, and hooves black. Paint tiny white commas on eyes. Highlight nose and hooves with lichen grey. Paint tiny lichen grey commas on hooves. Paint the space between the horns black.
3. Spray with a clear high-gloss acrylic finish.
4. Attach a sawtooth hanger on back. Assemble clock movement, numbers, and hands on the finished piece.

Copy pattern at 300%. Finished size: about 18" wide by 16½" high.

Fish #1 Clock

Painting and Finishing

1. Stain and seal whole surface.
2. Highlight with silver.
3. Paint eye straw and put a black dot in center with a small amount of straw showing around edge.
4. Triple-load a flat brush with coral, blue spruce, and silver to paint the fins. Put a coral wash on the tongue.
5. Spray with a clear high-gloss acrylic finish.
6. Attach 2 sawtooth hangers on back. Assemble clock movement, numbers, and hands on the finished piece.

Copy pattern at 245%. Finished size: about 21" wide by 7" high.

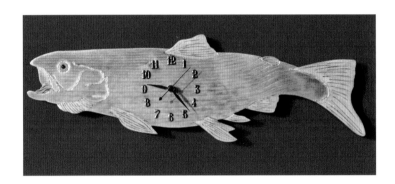

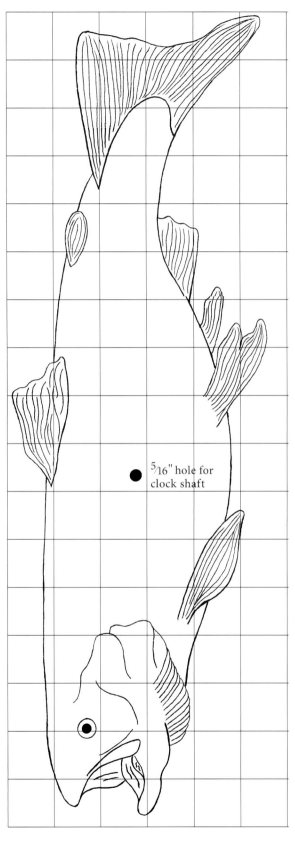

$^{5}/_{16}$" hole for clock shaft

Fish #2 Clock

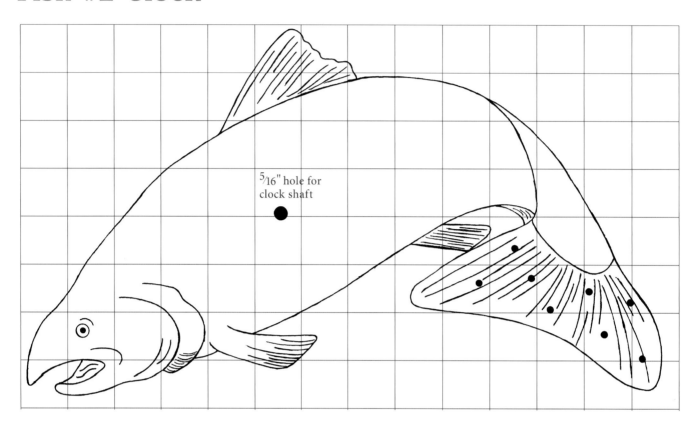

5/16" hole for clock shaft

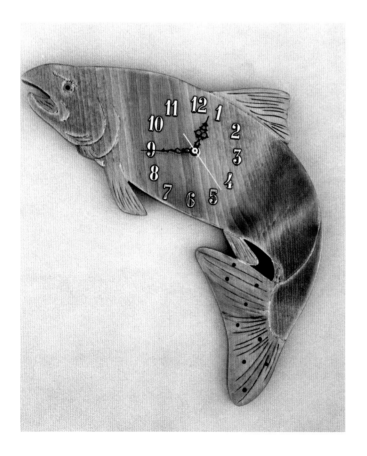

Painting and Finishing

1. Stain and seal whole surface.
2. Highlight with silver.
3. Paint eye straw and put a black dot in center with a small amount of straw showing around edge.
4. Triple-load a flat brush with coral, blue spruce, and silver to paint the fins. Put a coral wash on the tongue.
5. Put black dots on the tail. Paint black in the space between fins and tail.
6. Spray with a clear high-gloss acrylic finish.
7. Attach a sawtooth hanger on back. Assemble clock movement, numbers, and hands on the finished piece.

Copy pattern at 215%. Finished size: about 15" wide by 10½" high.

Deer Clock

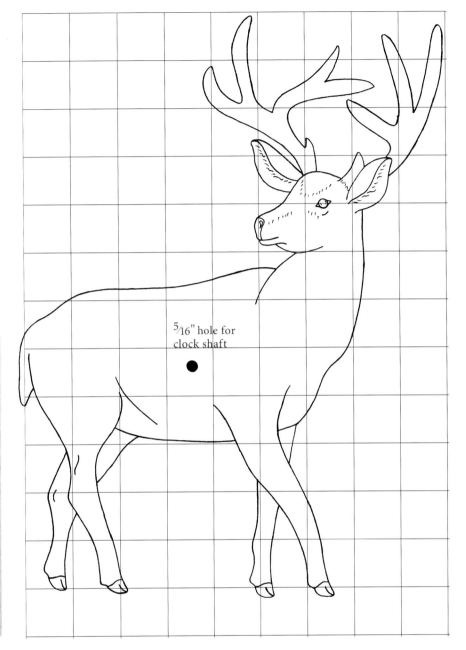

5⁄16" hole for
clock shaft

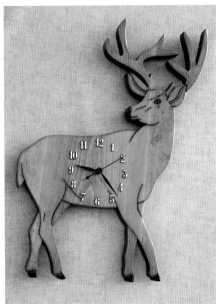

Painting and Finishing

1. Stain and seal whole surface. Shadow with brown velvet. Highlight with palomino tan.
2. Paint eyes, nose, and hooves black. Paint tiny white commas on eyes. Highlight nose and hooves with lichen grey. Paint tiny lichen grey commas on nose for nostril and also on hooves.
3. Spray with a clear high-gloss acrylic finish.
4. Attach a sawtooth hanger on back. Assemble clock movement, numbers, and hands on the finished piece.

Copy pattern at 235%. Finished size: about 12" wide by 15¾" high.

Fox Clock

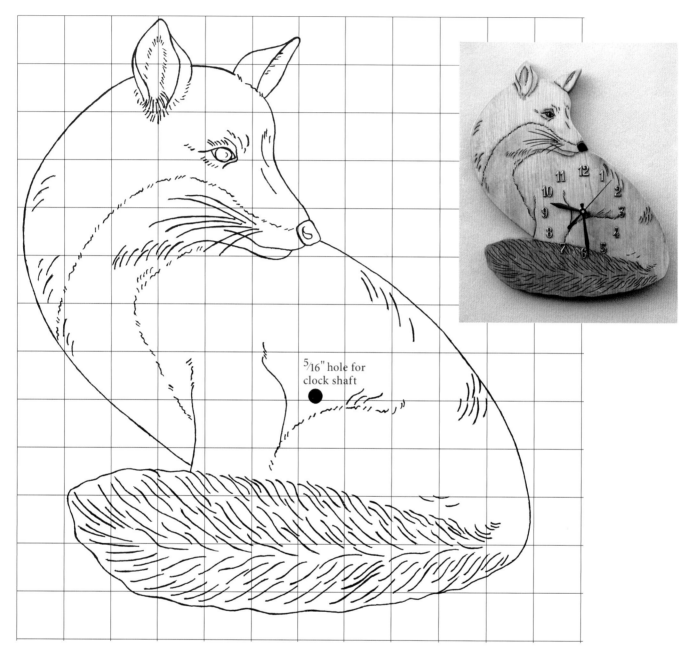

⁵/₁₆" hole for clock shaft

Painting and Finishing

1. Stain and seal whole surface. Shadow with brown velvet and highlight with palomino tan.

2. Paint eye and nose black. Paint tiny white comma on eye. Highlight nose with lichen grey.

3. Put a palomino tan wash on lower part of face, chin, neck and tummy. Put a burnt sienna wash on the tail.

4. Spray with a clear high-gloss acrylic finish.

5. Attach a sawtooth hanger on back. Assemble clock movement, numbers, and hands on the finished piece.

Copy pattern at 210%. Finished size: about 11½" wide by 12¾" high.

Squirrel Clock

5/16" hole for clock shaft

Painting and Finishing

1. Stain and seal whole surface.
2. Put a wash on the tail and end of acorn with burnt umber.
3. Shadow with brown velvet. Highlight with palomino tan.
4. Paint eye and nose black. Highlight nose with lichen grey. Paint tiny white commas on the eye.
5. Spray with a clear high-gloss acrylic finish.
6. Attach a sawtooth hanger on back. Assemble clock movement, numbers, and hands on the finished piece.

Copy pattern at 200%. Finished size: about 9¾" wide by 10½".

Rabbit Clock

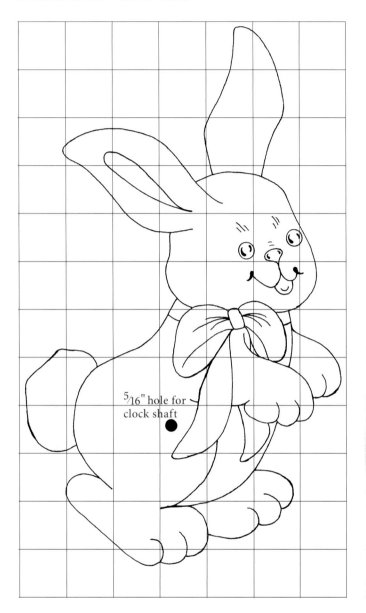

5/16" hole for clock shaft

Painting and Finishing

1. Stain and seal whole surface. Shadow with brown velvet. Highlight with palomino tan.
2. Paint eyes and nose black. Paint an upside-down white comma on the left side of each eye and a tiny comma on the other side. Paint tiny upside-down white commas on the nose for nostrils. Paint black eyelashes. Paint black comma on each side of mouth. Float adobe on the tongue and highlight with a tiny white comma.
3. Paint bow Wedgwood blue. Shadow with Cape Cod blue and highlight with blue mist. Paint gold commas on ends of ribbon and a tiny comma on the knot.
4. Spray with a clear high-gloss acrylic finish.
5. Attach a sawtooth hanger on back. Assemble clock movement, numbers, and hands on the finished piece.

Copy pattern at 240%. Finished size: about 8½" wide by 14" tall.

Elk Clock

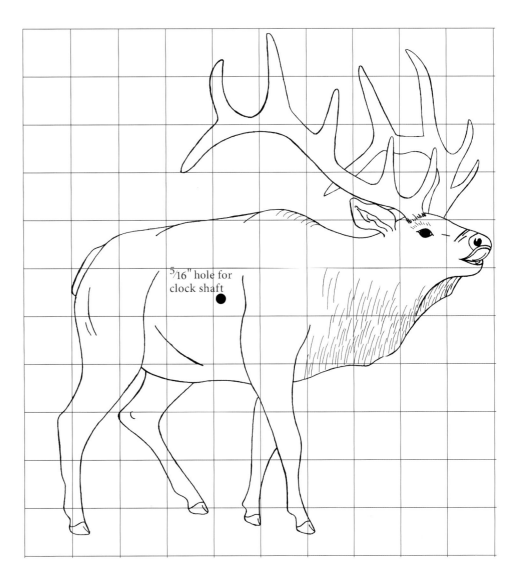

5/16" hole for clock shaft

Painting and Finishing

1. Stain and seal whole surface. Shadow with brown velvet and highlight with palomino tan.
2. Paint eye, nose, and hooves black. Paint tiny white comma on eye. Paint space between horns black.
3. Float brown velvet inside mouth. Highlight nose and hooves with lichen grey. Paint tiny lichen grey commas on hooves.
4. Spray with a clear high-gloss acrylic finish.
5. Attach a sawtooth hanger on back. Assemble clock movement, numbers, and hands on the finished piece.

Copy pattern at 300%. Finished size: about 14¼" wide by 16" high.

Perched Eagle Clock

5/16" hole for clock shaft

The eagle pictured is made from ¾" birch plywood, stained with American walnut.

Painting and Finishing

1. Stain and seal whole surface. Shadow with brown velvet and highlight with palomino tan.
2. Paint the beak and feet straw. Shadow with antique gold and highlight with ivory. Paint the toenails antique gold.
3. Paint the eye straw. Put a black dot on top, letting a small amount of straw show around the edges. Place a smaller black dot in center.
4. Put a wash on the log using burnt umber. Shadow with burnt umber and highlight with palomino tan.
5. Spray with a clear high-gloss acrylic finish.
6. Attach two sawtooth hangers on back. Assemble clock movement, numbers, and hands on the finished piece.

Copy pattern at 385%. Finished size: about 27" wide by 16" high.

Flying Eagle Clock

5/16" hole for
clock shaft

Painting and Finishing

1. Stain and seal whole surface. Shadow with brown velvet. Highlight with palomino tan.
2. Paint the eye, beak, and feet straw. Shadow with antique gold and highlight with antique white. Paint a small antique gold comma on the beak for the nostril. Put a black dot on the center of the eye.
3. Attach two sawtooth hangers on back. Assemble clock movement, numbers, and hands on the finished piece.

Copy pattern at 340%. Finished size: about 23½" wide by 17" high.

Eagle Head Clock

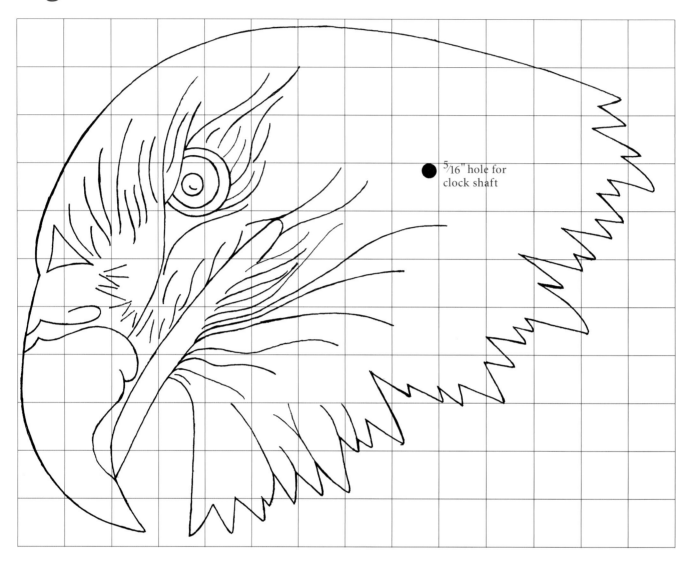

5/16" hole for clock shaft

Painting and Finishing

1. Stain and seal whole surface. Shadow with brown velvet and highlight with palomino tan.
2. Paint the beak straw. Shadow with antique gold and highlight with ivory. Paint the center dot of the eye black, straw around the black, then black around the straw.
3. Spray with a clear high-gloss acrylic finish.
4. Attach a sawtooth hanger on back. Assemble clock movement, numbers, and hands on the finished piece.

Copy pattern at 220%. Finished size: about 15" wide by 11" high.

Flying Duck Clock

5/16" hole for clock shaft

Painting and Finishing

1. Stain and seal whole surface. Shadow with brown velvet and highlight with palomino tan.
2. Paint eye, ring around neck, beak, and feet straw. Shadow with antique gold and highlight with antique white. Put a black dot on the eye.
3. Paint the end of the beak and tail black. Highlight with lichen grey.
4. Paint head black green. Shadow with black. Highlight with village green or mint green.
5. Spray with a clear high-gloss acrylic finish.
6. Attach a sawtooth hanger on back. Assemble clock movement, numbers, and hands on the finished piece.

Copy pattern at 270%. Finished size: about 18" wide by 14" high.

Mallard Duck Clock

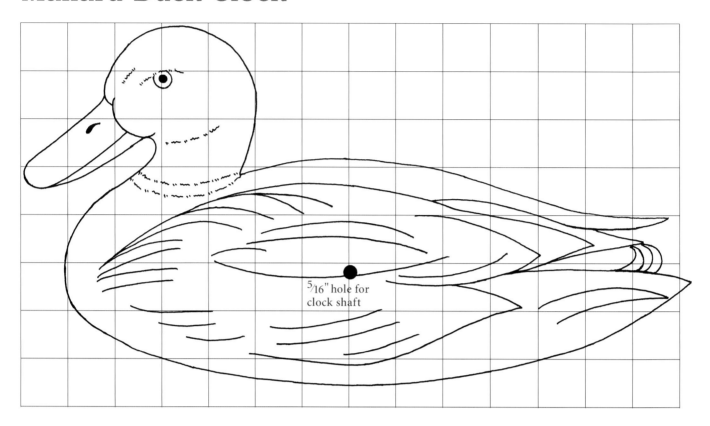

$^{5}/16$" hole for clock shaft

Painting and Finishing

1. Stain and seal whole surface. Shadow with brown velvet and highlight with palomino tan.
2. Paint eye, ring around neck, and beak straw. Shadow with antique gold and highlight with antique white. Paint a small comma stroke with antique gold on the beak for the nostril. Put a black dot in center of eye.
3. Paint head black green. Shadow with black and highlight with village green or mint green. Paint curled-up tail feathers black.
4. Spray with a clear high-gloss acrylic finish.
5. Attach a sawtooth hanger on back. Assemble clock movement, numbers, and hands on the finished piece.

Copy pattern at 250%. Finished size: about 15½" wide by 8¼" high.

Penguin Clock

Painting and Finishing

1. Stain back side and seal both sides.

2. Paint underside of wing and breast white. It will take about 6 coats to make it look right. Using the sponge brush helps make the job go faster. Finish it off by using an old frayed brush and dabbing the last coat of white.

3. Paint the underside of the beak and the side panel on the head pumpkin. Highlight with antique white. Shadow with tangerine.

4. Paint the rest of the penguin black. Highlight with lichen grey. Be sure to highlight the eyeball to make it stand out.

5. Spray with a clear high-gloss acrylic finish.

6. Attach a sawtooth hanger on back. Assemble clock movement, numbers, and hands on the finished piece.

Copy the pattern at 225%. Finished size: about 9½" wide by 15½" high.

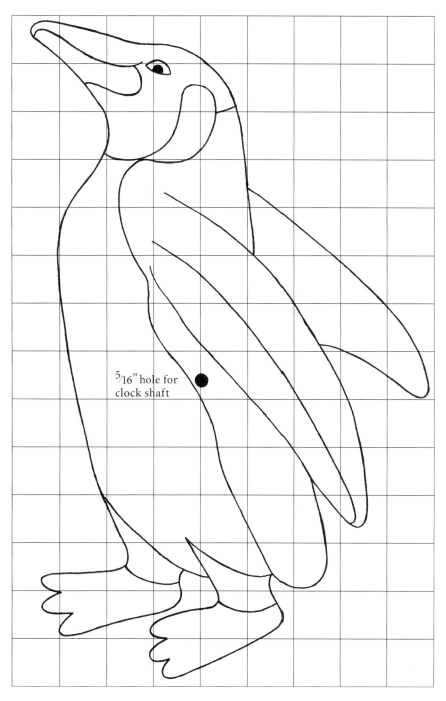

5⁄16" hole for clock shaft

Owl Clock

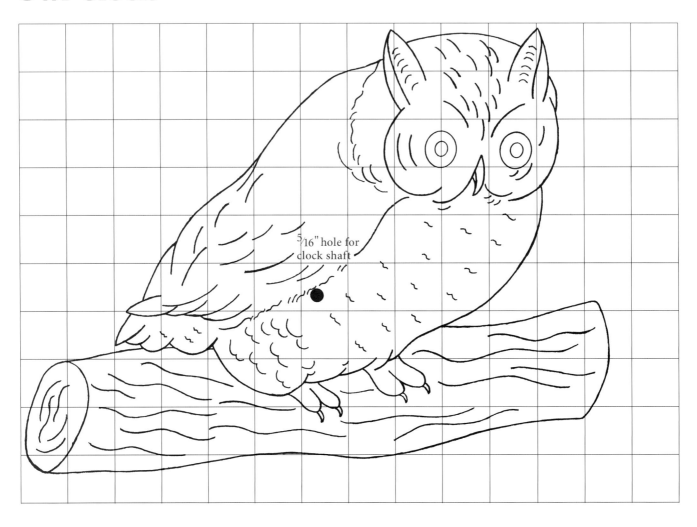

5/16" hole for clock shaft

Painting and Finishing

1. Stain and seal whole surface. Shadow with brown velvet. Highlight with palomino tan.
2. Paint the center of the eyes black. Paint the outer circle of the eye straw. Paint the beak and feet straw. Shadow with antique gold and highlight with antique white. Paint the toenails antique gold.
3. Put a wash on the log using burnt umber. Shadow with burnt umber and highlight with palomino tan.
4. Spray with a clear high-gloss acrylic finish.
5. Attach a sawtooth hanger on back. Assemble clock movement, numbers, and hands on the finished piece.

Copy pattern at 225%. Finished size: about 14" wide by 10¼" high.

Jumping Lamb Clock

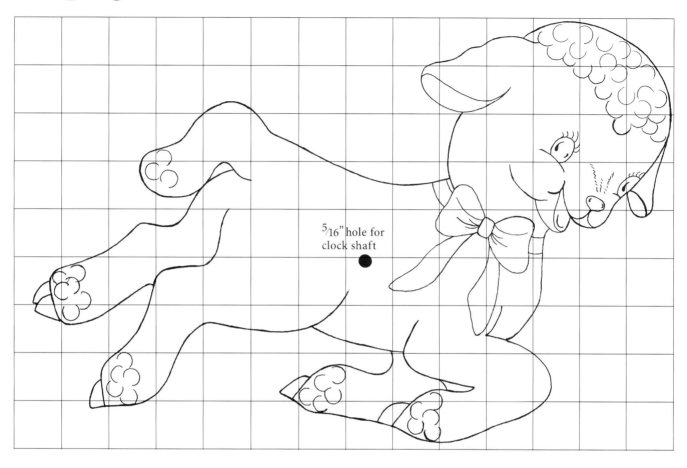

5/16" hole for clock shaft

Painting and Finishing

1. Stain with Puritan pine stain and seal whole surface. Shadow with brown velvet. Highlight with palomino tan.
2. Paint eyes, nose, and hooves black. Highlight hooves with lichen grey. Paint white upside-down commas on the left side of the eye and a tiny white comma on the other side. Paint tiny upside-down commas on the nose for nostrils. Paint black eyelashes. Paint black commas for eyebrows.
3. Float adobe on the tongue and cheeks. Highlight with tiny white commas.
4. Paint the bow Indiana rose. Shadow with gypsy rose and highlight with white. Paint gold commas on each end of the ribbon and a tiny comma on the knot.
5. Side-load a flat brush with antique white to paint the curls on head, tail, and feet.
6. Spray with a clear high-gloss acrylic finish.
7. Attach a sawtooth hanger on back. Assemble clock movement, numbers, and hands on the finished piece.

Copy pattern at 230%. Finished size: about 15¾" wide by 10½" tall.

Standing Lamb Clock

5/16" hole for clock shaft

The lamb clock pictured is made with ¾" birch plywood, stained with American walnut.

Painting and Finishing

1. Stain and seal whole surface. Shadow with brown velvet. Highlight with palomino tan.
2. Paint eyes, nose, and hooves black. Highlight nose and hooves with lichen grey. Paint white upside-down comma on the left side of the eye and a tiny white comma on the other side. Paint tiny upside-down comma on the nose for nostril. Paint black eyelashes. Paint a black comma for the brow and at edge of mouth.
3. Paint the bow sunbright yellow. Shadow with straw and highlight with white. Paint a gold comma on the end of the ribbon and a tiny comma on the knot. Paint the bell gold.
4. Side-load a flat brush with antique white to paint the curls on head, tail, ears, and feet.
5. Spray with a clear high-gloss acrylic finish.
6. Attach a sawtooth hanger on back. Assemble clock movement, numbers, and hands on the finished piece.

Copy pattern at 250%. Finished size: about 11" wide by 16" tall.

Piggy at Fence Clock

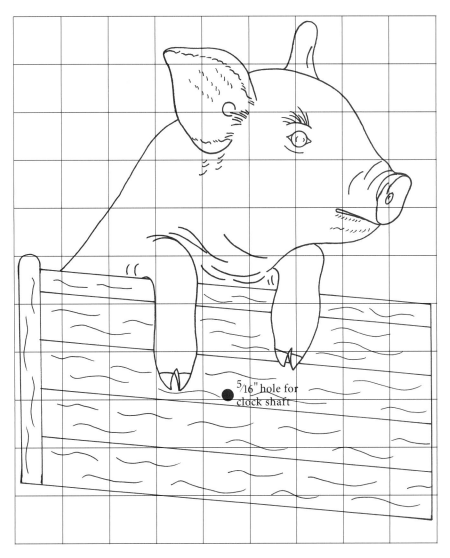

5/16" hole for clock shaft

Painting and Finishing

1. Stain and seal whole surface. Shadow with brown velvet. Highlight with palomino tan.
2. Put a wash on the fence with burnt umber.
3. Paint eye and hooves black. Highlight hooves with lichen grey. Paint tiny white commas on eye.
4. Spray with a clear high-gloss acrylic finish.
5. Attach a sawtooth hanger on back. Assemble clock movement, numbers, and hands on the finished piece.

Copy pattern at 250%. Finished size: about 11" wide by 12¾" tall.

Piggy with Shawl Clock

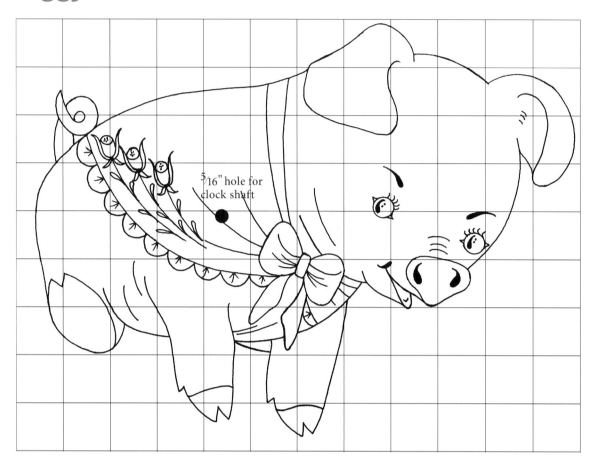

5/16" hole for clock shaft

Painting and Finishing

1. Stain and seal whole surface. Shadow with brown velvet and highlight with palomino tan.
2. Paint eyes black and put a white upside-down comma stroke on left side of eyes with a tiny comma on right side.
3. Paint hooves and inside of curl in tail black. Highlight hooves with lichen grey. Paint black comma strokes on the nose for nostrils, eyebrows, and at edge of mouth. Paint black eyelashes. Float adobe on inside of mouth and put a tiny white comma stroke to highlight.
4. Paint shawl in bouquet (a dusty rose color). Highlight with white and shadow with rose mist. Paint bow heritage blue. Shadow with nightfall blue and highlight with blue mist. Double-load a flat brush with blue mist and heritage blue to make the lace around edge of shawl, and paint the flowers. Double-load filbert brush with dark jungle green and Seminole green to paint the leaves. Put tiny gold commas on knot of bow and paint gold commas on ends of bow and around the lace. Using the

liner brush, pull heritage blue lines on the lace ruffles.
5. Spray with a clear high-gloss acrylic finish.
6. Attach a sawtooth hanger on back. Assemble clock movement, numbers, and hands on the finished piece.

Copy pattern at 210%. Finished size: about 12" wide by 12½" high.

Plump Piggy Clock

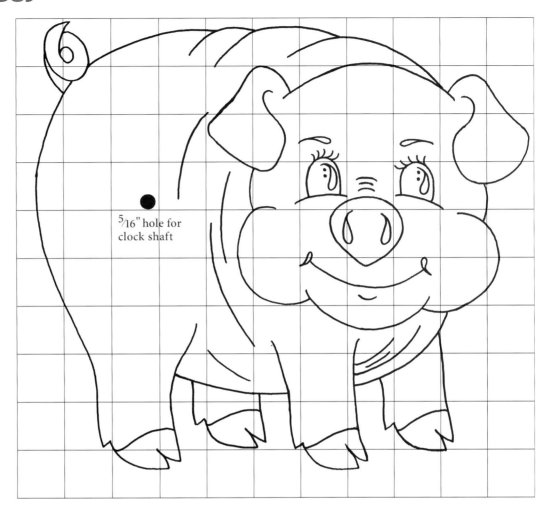

5⁄16" hole for clock shaft

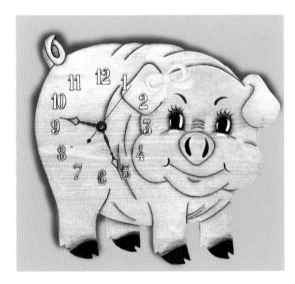

Painting and Finishing

1. Stain and seal whole surface. Shadow with brown velvet and highlight with palomino tan.
2. Paint eyes black and put a white upside-down comma stroke on right side of eyes with a tiny comma on left side.
3. Paint hooves and inside of curl in tail black. Highlight hooves with lichen grey.
4. Paint black comma strokes for nostrils, eyebrows, and at edges of mouth. Paint black eyelashes.
5. Side-load adobe on cheeks and highlight with tiny white comma strokes.
6. Paint a bow by the ear for a little extra color using Wedgwood blue. Shadow with Cape Cod blue and highlight with blue mist. Paint gold commas on ends of bow.
7. Spray with a clear high-gloss acrylic finish.
8. Attach a sawtooth hanger on back. Assemble clock movement, numbers, and hands on the finished piece.

Copy pattern at 225%. Finished size: about 12" wide by 10½" high.

Hen Clock

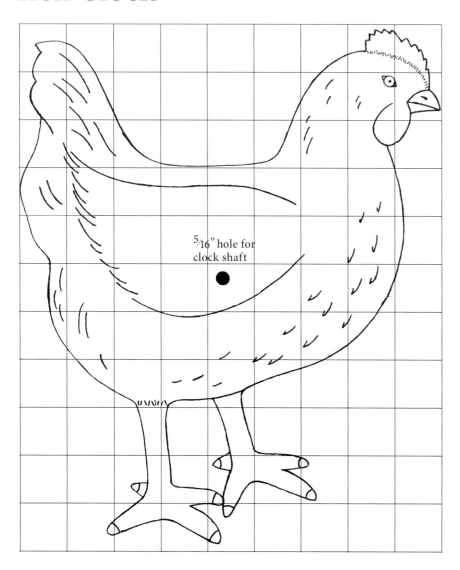

⁵/₁₆" hole for clock shaft

Painting and Finishing

1. Stain and seal whole surface. Shadow with brown velvet and highlight with palomino tan.

2. Paint beak, eye, and feet straw. Shadow with antique gold and highlight with antique white. Paint the toes antique gold. Paint a tiny antique gold comma on the beak for a nostril. Put a black dot in the middle of the eye.

3. Paint the comb and wattle tomato spice. Highlight with Indiana rose.

4. Spray with a clear high-gloss acrylic finish.

5. Attach a sawtooth hanger to the back. Assemble clock movement, numbers, and hands on the finished piece.

Copy pattern at 225%. Finished size: about 10¼" wide by 12" high.

Rooster Clock

5/16" hole for clock shaft

Painting and Finishing

1. Stain and seal whole surface. Shadow with brown velvet and highlight with palomino tan.
2. Paint beak and feet straw. Shadow with antique gold and highlight with antique white. Paint the toes antique gold. Paint a tiny antique gold comma on the beak for a nostril. Paint the outer part of the eye white and the smaller part straw. Then put a black dot on the straw.
3. Paint the comb and wattle tomato spice. Highlight with Indiana rose.
4. Put a liberty blue wash on the tail feathers. Shadow with liberty blue and highlight with blue mist. Paint the space between legs black.
5. Spray with a clear high-gloss acrylic finish.
6. Attach a sawtooth hanger to the back. Assemble clock movement, numbers, and hands on the finished piece.

Copy pattern at 225%. Finished size: about 10½" wide by 13" high.

Dairy Cow Clock

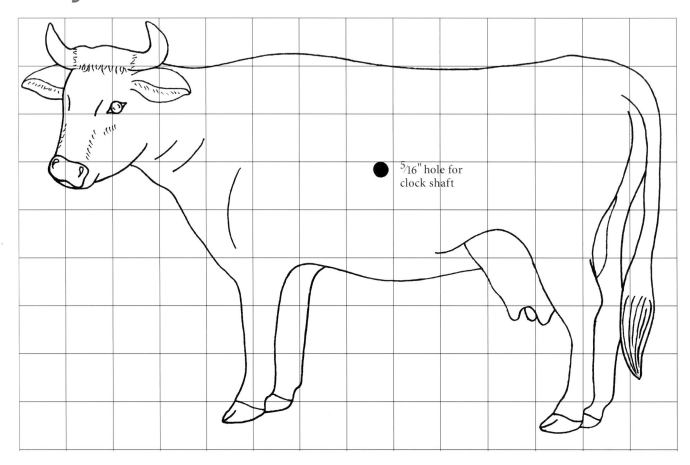

5/16" hole for clock shaft

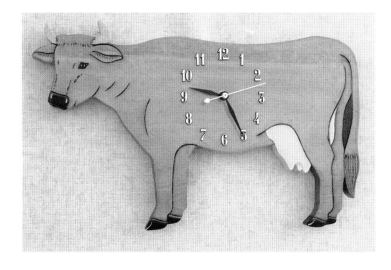

Painting and Finishing

1. Stain and seal whole surface. Shadow with brown velvet. Highlight with palomino tan.
2. Paint horns lichen grey and highlight with white. Paint light lines on horns with white.
3. Paint nose, eye, and hooves black. Highlight with lichen grey. Paint tiny upside-down commas on hooves and nose for nostrils and split hooves with lichen grey. Paint tiny white commas on eye.
4. Paint udder fleshtone. Shadow with medium flesh. Highlight with white.
5. Spray with a clear high-gloss acrylic finish.
6. Attach a sawtooth hanger on back. Assemble clock movement, numbers, and hands on the finished piece.

Copy pattern at 200%. Finished size: about 13¾" wide by 8½" high.

Bull Clock

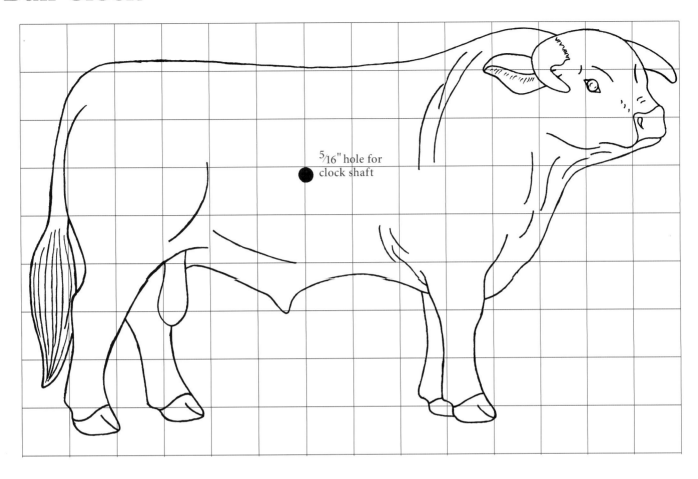

⁵/₁₆" hole for clock shaft

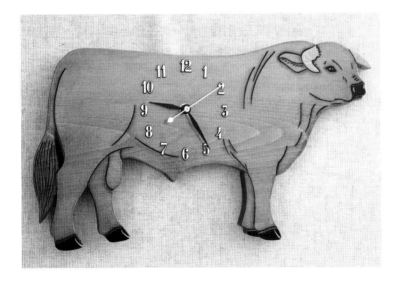

Painting and Finishing

1. Stain and seal whole surface. Shadow with brown velvet. Highlight with palomino tan.
2. Paint horns lichen grey. Highlight with white and paint light white lines on the horns.
3. Paint nose, eye, and hooves black. Highlight with lichen grey and paint upside-down commas on nose and hooves for nostrils and split hooves. Paint tiny white commas on eye.
4. Spray with a clear high-gloss acrylic finish.
5. Attach a sawtooth hanger on back. Assemble clock movement, numbers, and hands on the finished piece.

Copy pattern at 200%. Finished size: about 14" wide by 8¼" high.

Cow with Red Bows Clock

$^{5}/_{16}$" hole for clock shaft

The cow clock pictured is made with ¾" birch plywood, stained with American walnut.

Painting and Finishing

1. Stain and seal whole surface. Shadow with brown velvet and highlight with palomino tan.
2. Float brown velvet on hair on top of head and end of tail. Shadow upper eyelids and inside nostrils with brown velvet.
3. Paint eyes and hooves black. Paint tiny white commas on eyes. Highlight hooves with lichen grey. Paint tiny upside-down commas on hooves with lichen grey.
4. Paint udder fleshtone. Shadow with medium flesh and highlight with ivory. Paint the small spaces between back legs under udder, between bow and tail, and bow and chin black. Paint hairs at base of ears and eyelashes black.
5. Paint the bell gold. Paint horns lichen grey and highlight with white. Put light lines on the horns with white. Paint bows tomato spice. Shadow with maroon. Highlight with Indiana rose.
6. Spray with a clear high-gloss acrylic finish.
7. Attach a sawtooth hanger on back. Assemble clock movement, numbers, and hands on the finished piece.

Copy pattern at 195%. Finished size: about 12" wide by 10½" high.

Cowgirl Clock

The Cowgirl Clock pictured is made with ¾" birch plywood, stained with American walnut.

Painting and Finishing

1. Stain and seal the whole surface. Shadow with brown velvet and highlight with palomino tan.
2. Paint eyes and hooves black. Paint tiny white commas on eyes. Highlight hooves with lichen grey. Paint upside-down commas on hooves with lichen grey.
3. Paint udder fleshtone. Shadow with medium flesh and highlight with ivory.
4. Paint black comma strokes for the nostrils and at edge of mouth. Also use black for the small spaces between back legs under udder, between bow and tail, and bow and chin. Paint hairs at base of ears and eyelashes black.
5. Paint the bell gold. Paint hat and bows heritage blue. Shadow with midnight blue and highlight with Wedgwood blue.
6. Spray with a clear high-gloss acrylic finish.
7. Attach a sawtooth hanger on back. Assemble clock movement, numbers, and hands on the finished piece.

Copy pattern at 225%. Finished size: about 15½" wide by 14" high.

⁵⁄₁₆" hole for clock shaft

Duck with Hat Clock

5/16" hole for clock shaft

Painting and Finishing

1. Stain and seal whole surface. Shadow with brown velvet, highlight with palomino tan.
2. Paint the beak and feet straw. Shadow with antique gold and highlight with antique white. Paint a tiny antique gold comma on the beak for a nostril.
3. Float adobe under the eye and highlight with a tiny white comma. Paint the eye black. Paint a white upside-down comma on the right side and a tiny comma on the left. Paint black eyelashes.
4. Paint antique white comma strokes to detail the wing and tail.
5. Paint the hat and the bow around the neck Wedgwood blue. Shadow with Cape Cod blue and highlight with blue mist. Paint the bow on the hat heritage blue. Shadow with nightfall blue and highlight with Wedgwood blue. Put groups of dots on the upper hat and bow around the neck. Paint gold commas on the end of the bows and tiny gold commas on the knots.
6. Paint the space between the legs black.
7. Spray with a clear high-gloss acrylic finish.
8. Attach a sawtooth hanger to the back. Assemble clock movement, numbers, and hands on the finished piece.

Copy pattern at 225%. Finished size: about 9" wide by 16" high.

Susie Goose Clock

Painting and Finishing

1. Stain and seal whole surface. Shadow with brown velvet and highlight with palomino tan.
2. Paint the beak and feet straw. Shadow with antique gold and highlight with antique white. Paint nostril antique gold.
3. Paint the eye and lashes black. Paint an upside-down comma on the left side of the eye with white and a tiny comma on the right. Float adobe under the eye and highlight with a tiny white comma.
4. Paint antique white comma strokes on the wing and tail to detail.
5. Paint the hat and bow Wedgwood blue. Shadow with Cape Cod blue and highlight with blue mist. Paint the band on the hat gold. Paint gold commas on the end of the ribbon and on the knot. Put groups of dots on the top of the hat and bow with blue mist.
6. Spray with a clear high-gloss acrylic finish.
7. Attach a sawtooth hanger to the back. Assemble clock movement, numbers, and hands on the finished piece.

Copy pattern at 220%. Finished size: about 9½" wide by 15" high.

Goose on Barrel Clock

5⁄16" hole for clock shaft

Painting and Finishing

1. Stain and seal whole surface. Shadow the barrel with brown velvet and highlight with palomino tan.
2. Paint several coats of white on the goose. Daub the last coat of white on with an old frayed brush. Do not get the daubing on the shawl or hat.
3. Paint the beak straw. Shadow with antique gold and highlight with antique white. Paint a small comma stroke on the beak with antique gold for the nostril.
4. Paint comma strokes on the tail with antique white. Paint the eye black. Paint an upside-down comma on the left side with white and a tiny comma on the left side. Paint black eyelashes. Float adobe under the eye and paint a tiny white comma to highlight.
5. Paint the hat and shawl in bouquet (a dusty rose color). Shadow with rose mist and highlight with white. Paint the ruffle on the barrel rose mist.

Shadow with candy bar brown and highlight with bouquet. Paint the bow heritage blue. Shadow with midnight blue and highlight with blue mist. Double-load a flat brush with heritage blue and blue mist to make the lace around the edge of the shawl. With a liner brush, pull lines in each scallop to make it look ruffled. Paint the band on the hat gold. Paint gold commas around the edge of the ruffled lace. Paint gold commas on the ends of the ribbon and tiny gold commas on the knot. Paint tiny gold commas around shawl where the lace is attached. Double-load brush with heritage blue and blue mist for the flowers. Double-load brush with Seminole green and dark jungle green for the leaves. Put groups of dots on the top of the hat and on the ruffle the goose is sitting on.
6. Paint black on the rims of the barrel.
7. Spray with a clear high-gloss acrylic finish.
8. Attach a sawtooth hanger to the back. Assemble clock movement, numbers, and hands on the finished piece.

Copy pattern at 280%. Finished size: about 9½" wide by 15" high.

Sundae Clock

Painting and Finishing

1. Stain and seal whole surface. Shadow the dish with brown velvet and highlight with palomino tan. Put a brown velvet wash on the 3 indented-looking sections of the dish.
2. Paint the ice cream antique white. Shadow with maple sugar and highlight with white. Paint the topping dark chocolate and highlight with light chocolate.
3. Paint the cherries in tomato spice. Shadow with maroon and highlight with coral.
4. Spray with a clear high-gloss acrylic finish.
5. Attach a sawtooth hanger to the back. Assemble clock movement, numbers, and hands on the finished piece.

Copy pattern at 200%. Finished size: about 6¾" wide by 14½" high.

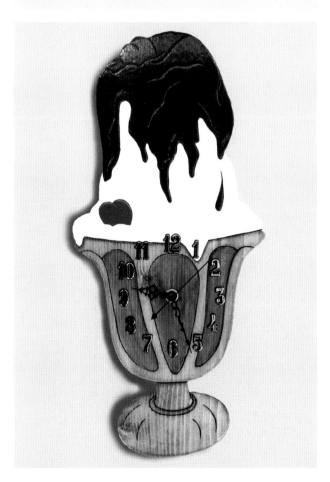

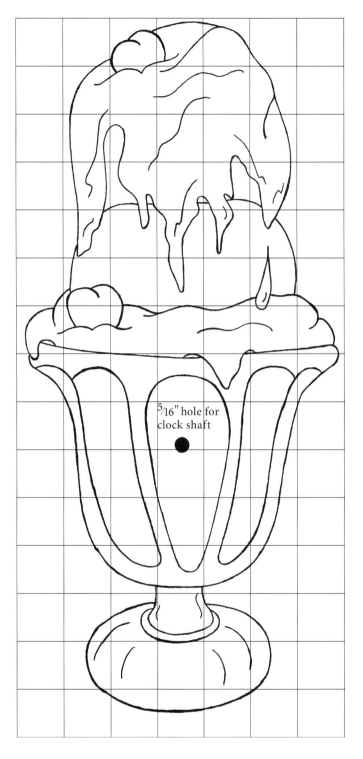

5/16" hole for clock shaft

Cornucopia Clock

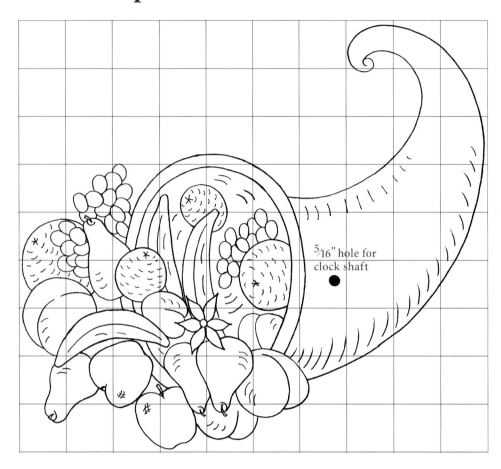

5⁄16" hole for clock shaft

Copy the pattern at 250%. Finished size: about 12¾" wide by 11½" high.

Painting and Finishing

1. Stain and seal whole surface. Shadow with brown velvet and highlight with palomino tan.
2. Paint the apples in tomato spice. Shadow with maroon. Highlight with Indiana rose. Paint the apple stem brown velvet.
3. Paint the peaches medium flesh. Shadow and make bright cheeks with Caucasian flesh (light adobe color). Highlight with antique white.
4. Paint the pears straw. Shadow with antique gold and highlight with antique white. Paint the stems brown velvet.
5. Paint the oranges in pumpkin. Highlight with antique white. Take an old frayed brush, dip in antique white and remove the excess; then lightly daub it on the orange.
6. Paint the bananas butter yellow. Shadow with antique gold and highlight with antique white.
7. Paint the plums vintage wine. Highlight with wisteria.
8. Paint the grapes in leprechaun (grayish green). Highlight with village green.
9. Paint the flower antique white with straw dot in the center.
10. Paint the spaces between the fruit outside the cornucopia black.
11. Spray with a clear high-gloss acrylic finish.
12. Attach a sawtooth hanger to the back. Assemble clock movement, numbers, and hands on the finished piece.

Strawberry Clock

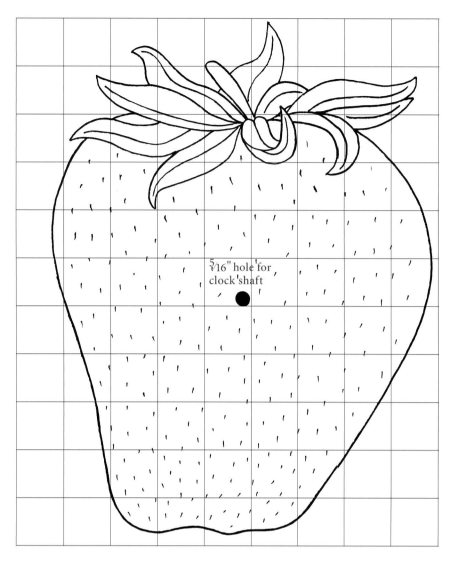

5⁄16" hole for clock shaft

Painting and Finishing

1. Stain the back side and seal both sides.
2. Paint the strawberry in tomato spice (bright red). Shadow with maroon. Highlight with Indiana rose. Paint the stem brown velvet. Highlight with palomino tan. Paint the leaves Seminole green. Double-load a flat brush with Seminole green and dark jungle green and paint over the underside (shadow side). Double-load a flat brush with Seminole and apple green and paint over the top side (highlight side). Paint the seeds straw.
3. Spray with a clear high-gloss acrylic finish.
4. Attach a sawtooth hanger to the back. Assemble clock movement, numbers, and hands on the finished piece.

Copy pattern at 205%. Finished size: about 8¼" wide by 11" high.

Apple Clock

5/16" hole for clock shaft

Painting and Finishing

1. Stain the back side and seal both sides.
2. Paint the apple in tomato spice (bright red). Shadow with maroon. Highlight with Indiana rose. Paint the bite in the apple antique white. Highlight with white. Paint the stem brown velvet. Highlight with palomino tan.
3. Paint the leaf Seminole green. Double-load a flat brush with Seminole green and dark jungle green and paint over the underside (shadow side). Double-load a flat brush with Seminole and apple green and paint over the top side (highlight side).
4. Spray with a clear high-gloss acrylic finish.
5. Attach a sawtooth hanger to the back. Assemble clock movement, numbers, and hands on the finished piece.

Copy pattern at 210%. Finished size: about 7¾" wide by 9½" high.

Basket of Potatoes Clock

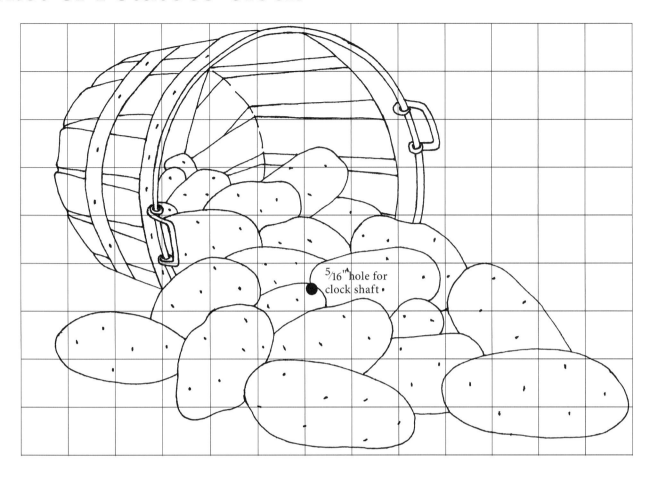

5/16" hole for clock shaft

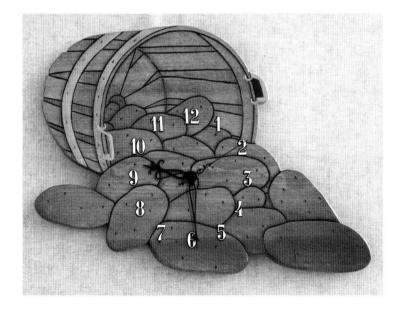

Painting and Finishing

1. Stain and seal whole surface.
2. Put a burnt umber wash on the potatoes. Shadow the potatoes and basket with brown velvet and highlight with palomino tan.
3. Put a turquoise wash on the two bands around the basket. Paint the handles lichen grey. Paint space inside the right handle black.
4. Spray with a clear high-gloss acrylic finish.
5. Attach a sawtooth hanger to the back. Assemble clock movement, numbers, and hands on the finished piece.

Copy pattern at 245%. Finished size: about 15" wide by 11" high.

Mushroom Clock

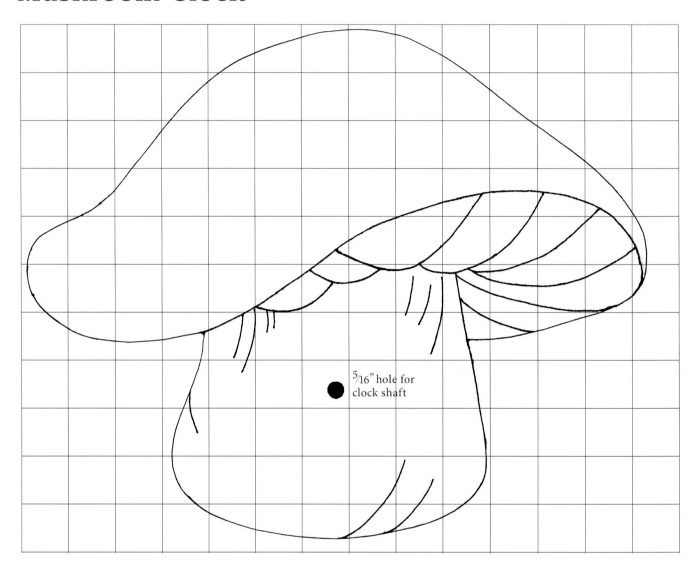

$^5/_{16}$" hole for clock shaft

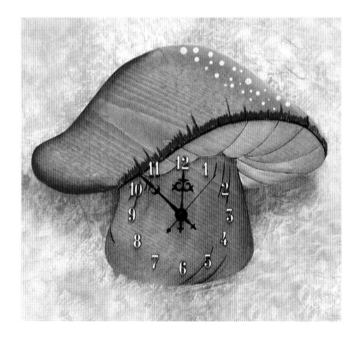

Painting and Finishing

1. Stain and seal whole surface. Shadow with brown velvet and highlight with palomino tan. Put a palomino tan wash on the underside of the top part.
2. Side-load a brush with burnt sienna and paint on the top of the wood-burned edge and left top. Put various sizes of dots on the right top with antique white.
3. Spray with a clear high-gloss acrylic finish.
4. Attach a sawtooth hanger to the back. Assemble clock movement, numbers, and hands on the finished piece.

Copy pattern at 200%. Finished size: about 13¼" wide by 10½" high.

Hamburger Clock

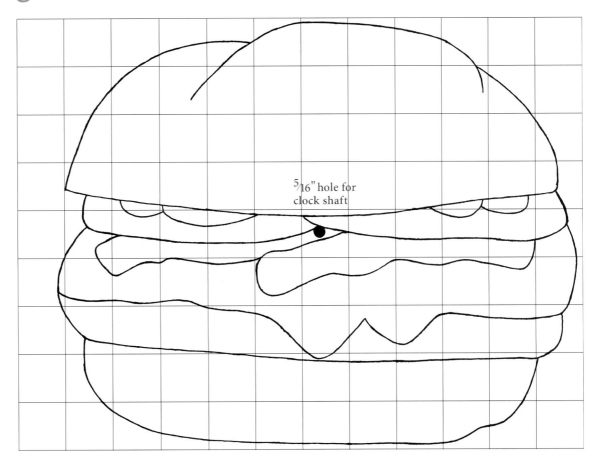

5/16" hole for clock shaft

Painting and Finishing

1. Stain and seal whole surface. Shadow with brown velvet and highlight with palomino tan.
2. Paint the tomatoes in tomato spice (bright red). Paint the onions antique white. Paint the cheese in butter yellow (or straw). Shadow with antique gold and highlight with antique white. Paint the ground beef burnt umber. Paint the bacon burnt sienna. Side-load a flat brush with antique white and make 2 wavy lines through each bacon strip.
3. Spray with a clear high-gloss acrylic finish.
4. Attach a sawtooth hanger to the back. Assemble clock movement, numbers, and hands on the finished piece.

Copy pattern at 250%. Finished size: about 13¾" wide by 11¼" high.

Ice Cream Cone Clock

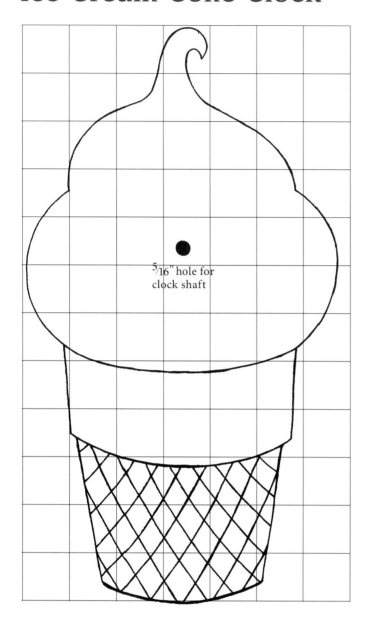

5/16" hole for
clock shaft

Painting and Finishing

1. Stain and seal whole surface. Shadow the cone with brown velvet and highlight with palomino tan.
2. Paint the ice cream antique white. Shadow with flesh tan and highlight with white.
3. Spray with a clear high-gloss acrylic finish.
4. Attach a sawtooth hanger to the back. Assemble clock movement, numbers, and hands on the finished piece.

Copy pattern at 200%. Finished size: about 6¾" wide by 12¼" high.

Breadboard Clock

Painting and Finishing

1. Stain and seal whole surface. Shadow with brown velvet and highlight with palomino tan.
2. Paint the knife blade in lichen grey. Highlight with white. Paint the knife handle brown velvet. Highlight with palomino tan.
3. Put a burnt sienna wash on the outside of the bread. Put a palomino tan wash on the inside of the loaf. Take an old frayed brush, dip in antique white, and remove excess; then daub lightly over the palomino tan wash.
4. Spray with a clear high-gloss acrylic finish.
5. Attach a sawtooth hanger to the back. Assemble clock movement, numbers, and hands on the finished piece.

Copy the pattern at 220%. Finished size: about 9¼" wide by 14¾" high.

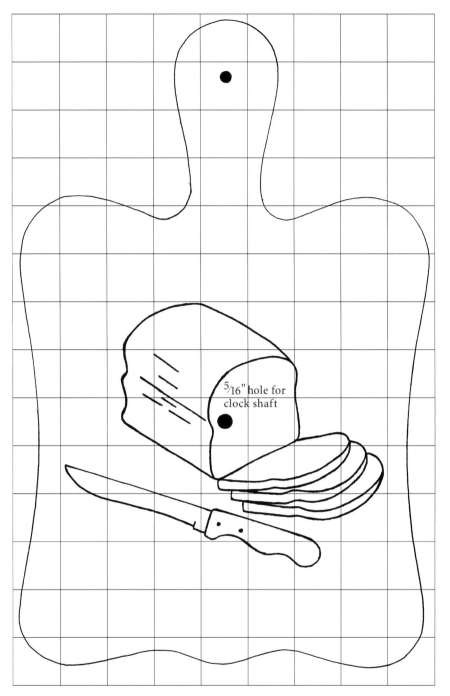

⁵⁄16" hole for clock shaft

Rolling Pin Clock

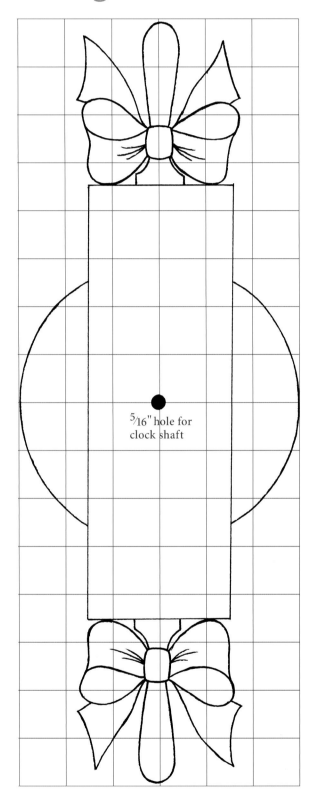

5/16" hole for clock shaft

Painting and Finishing

1. Stain and seal whole surface. Shadow with brown velvet and highlight with palomino tan.
2. Paint the bows Wedgwood blue. Shadow with Cape Cod blue and highlight with blue mist. Put gold commas on the ends of the ribbons.
3. Spray with a clear high-gloss acrylic finish.
4. Attach a sawtooth hanger to the back. Assemble clock movement, numbers, and hands on the finished piece.

Copy pattern at 200%. Finished size: about 16" wide by 6" high.

Milk Can Clock

Painting and Finishing

1. Stain and seal whole surface. Shadow with brown velvet and highlight with palomino tan.
2. Paint the space between the back handle and can black.
3. Paint flowers on top and bottom rims.
4. Spray with a clear high-gloss acrylic finish.
5. Attach a sawtooth hanger on back. Assemble clock movement, numbers, and hands on the finished piece.

Copy pattern at 210%. Finished size: about 7" wide by 15¼" tall.

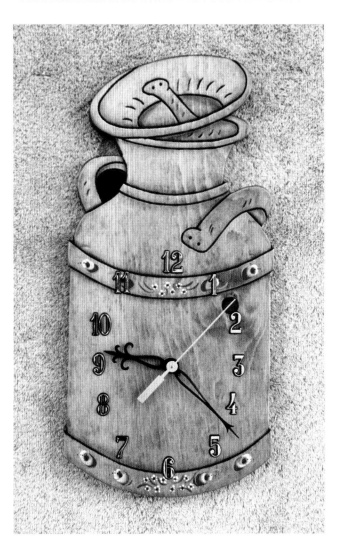

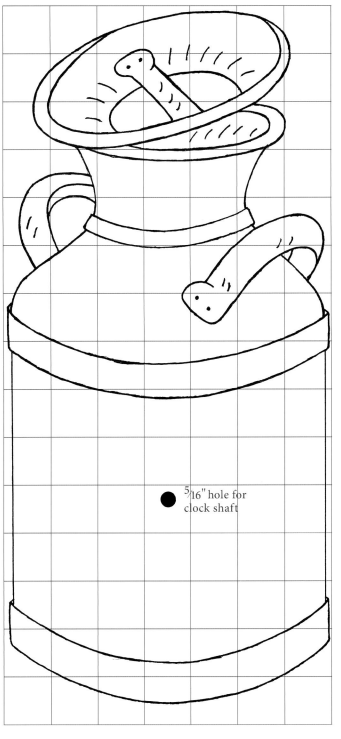

● ⁵/16" hole for clock shaft

Skier on Sun Clock

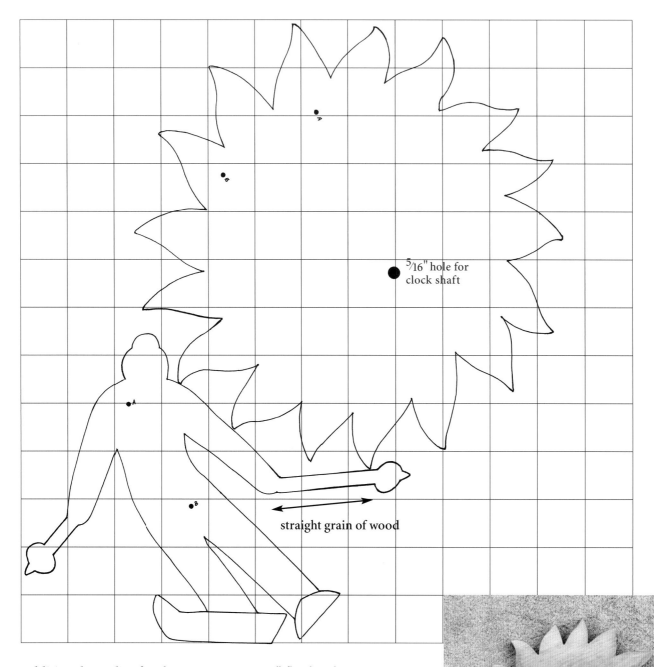

$^{5}/_{16}$" hole for
clock shaft

straight grain of wood

Additional supplies for this project: Two 1¼" flat-head screws.
The skier and sun are cut as two separate pieces.

Painting and Finishing

1. Stain sun and back side of skier in Puritan pine; seal both sides.
2. Paint the skier black. Highlight with lichen grey.
3. Spray each piece separately with a clear high-gloss acrylic finish.
4. When they are completely dry, attach the skier to the sun with 1½"
   flat-head screws, working from the back so the screws don't show.
5. Attach a sawtooth hanger on back. Assemble clock movement,
   numbers, and hands on the finished piece.

Copy pattern at 250%. Finished size: about 11½" diameter of
the sun. Skier is approximately 10½" wide by 8" high.

Baseball Clock

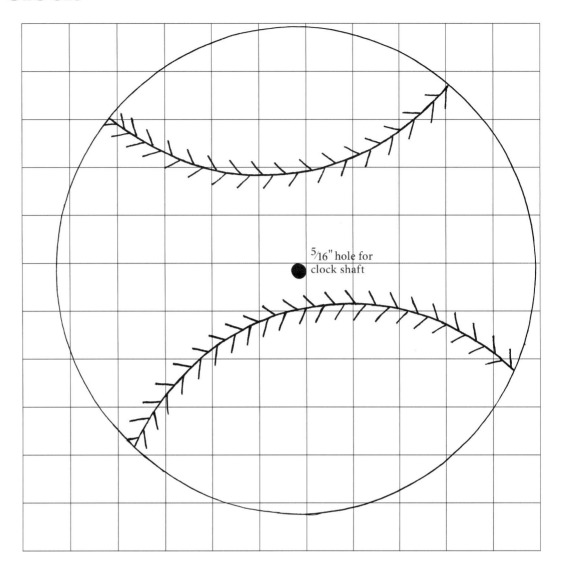

$^5/16$" hole for clock shaft

Painting and Finishing

1. Stain the back and seal both sides.
2. Paint several coats of white. Daub on the last coat with an old frayed brush.
3. Pull lichen grey in the sewn lines and tomato spice in the stitches.
4. Spray with a clear high-gloss acrylic finish.
5. Attach a sawtooth hanger on back. Assemble clock movement, numbers, and hands on the finished piece.

Copy pattern at 200%. Finished size: about 10" diameter.

Mitt and Baseball Clock

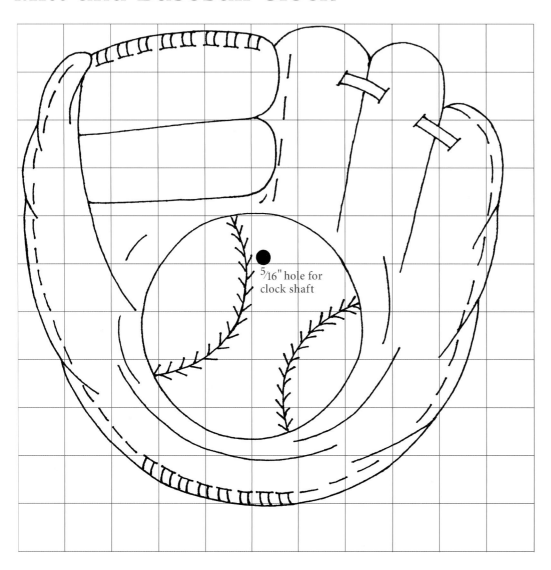

⁵⁄₁₆" hole for clock shaft

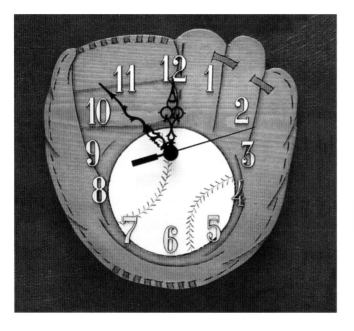

Painting and Finishing

1. Stain and seal whole surface. Shadow with brown velvet and highlight with palomino tan.
2. Paint the ball white. Pull the sewing lines with lichen grey. Paint the stitches tomato spice.
3. Spray with a clear high-gloss acrylic finish.
4. Attach a sawtooth hanger on back. Assemble clock movement, numbers, and hands on the finished piece.

Copy pattern at 195%. Finished size: about 10" wide by 10" tall.

Soccer Ball Clock

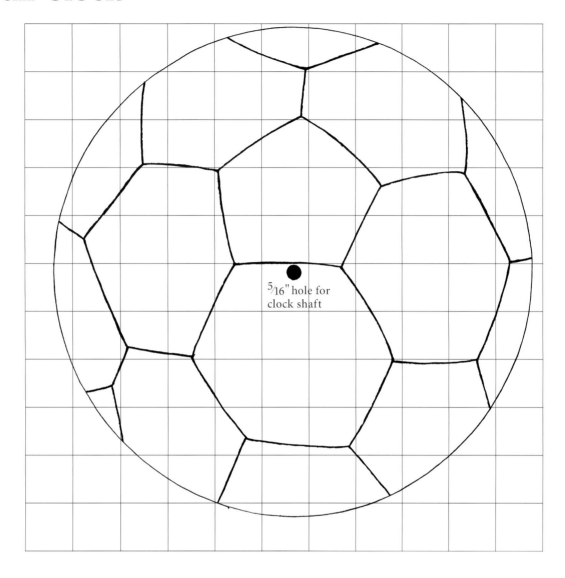

$^5/_{16}$" hole for clock shaft

Painting and Finishing

1. Stain the back and seal both sides.
2. Paint black and white as pictured. Pull black lines through all the lines.
3. Spray with a clear high-gloss acrylic finish.
4. Attach a sawtooth hanger on back. Assemble clock movement, numbers, and hands on the finished piece.

Copy pattern at 200%. Finished size: about 10" diameter.

Basketball Clock

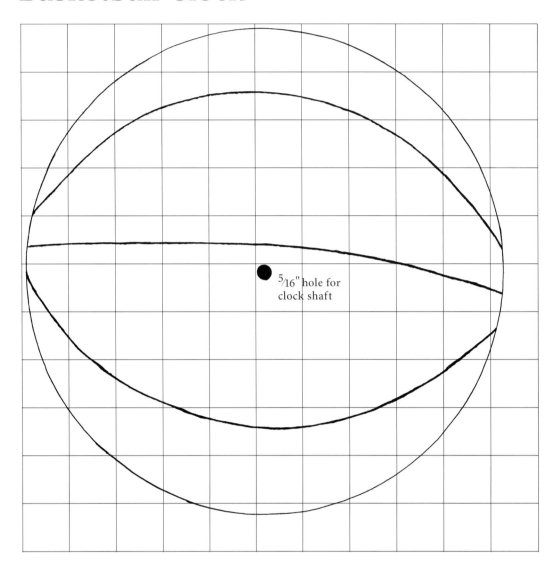

$5/16$" hole for clock shaft

Painting and Finishing

1. Stain and seal whole surface. Shadow with brown velvet and highlight with palomino tan.
2. Spray with a clear high-gloss acrylic finish.
3. Attach a sawtooth hanger on back. Assemble clock movement, numbers, and hands on the finished piece.

Copy pattern at 195%. Finished size: about 10" diameter.

Football Clock

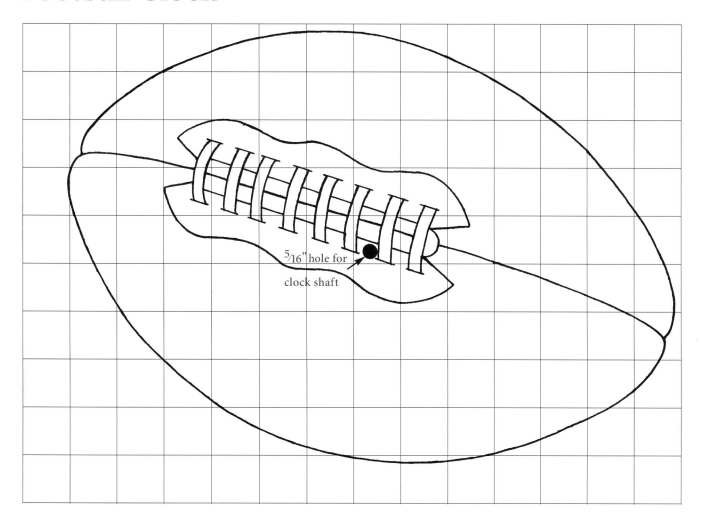

$5/16$" hole for
clock shaft

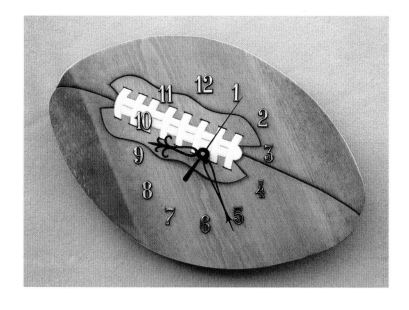

Painting and Finishing

1. Stain and seal whole surface. Shadow with brown velvet and highlight with palomino tan.
2. Paint lacing antique white. Shadow with palomino tan. Highlight with white.
3. Spray with a clear high-gloss acrylic finish.
4. Attach a sawtooth hanger on back. Assemble clock movement, numbers, and hands on the finished piece.

Copy pattern at 200%. Finished size: about 13" wide by 8¾" tall.

Bowling Pin and Ball Clock

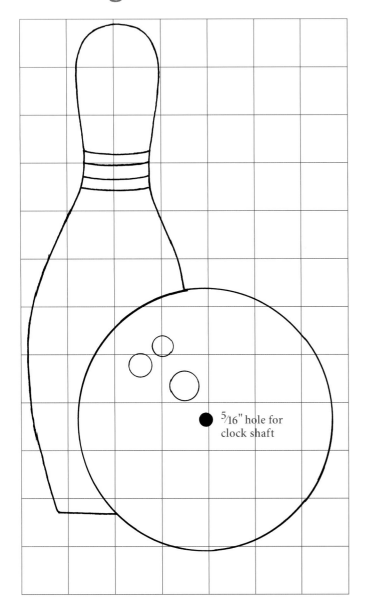

5/16" hole for clock shaft

Painting and Finishing

1. Stain the back and seal both sides.
2. Paint the pin with several coats of white. Daub on the last coat with an old frayed brush. Paint tomato spice stripes on the pin.
3. Paint the ball Wedgwood blue. Shadow with Cape Cod blue and highlight with blue mist.
4. Spray with a clear high-gloss acrylic finish.
5. Attach a sawtooth hanger on back. Assemble clock movement, numbers, and hands on the finished piece.

Copy pattern at 220%. Finished size: about 7¼" wide by 12" high.

Three Pins and Bowling Ball Clock

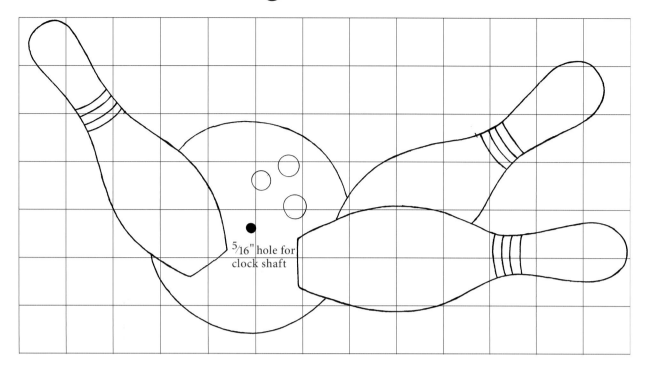

$^5/_{16}$" hole for clock shaft

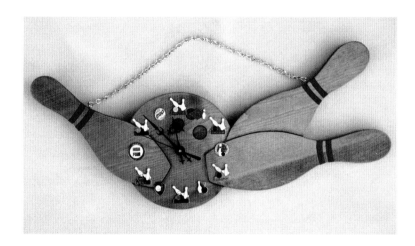

Additional supplies for this project:

• 14" gold- or silver-toned chain
• 2 small gold- or silver-toned eye screws

Painting and Finishing

1. Stain and seal whole surface. Shadow with brown velvet and highlight with palomino tan.

2. Paint tomato spice on the stripes of the pins.

3. Spray with a clear high-gloss acrylic finish.

4. Drill small holes and screw in the eye screws on top edge of wood between stripes, as shown; attach a 14" chain to the eye screws for the hanger.

5. Assemble clock movement, numbers, and hands on the finished piece. If you have a lot of pins and would like to display them, here is a good way. Take the backs off and hot-glue a different pin for each number or just for the 3, 6, 9, and 12 numbers.

Copy pattern at 270%. Finished size: about 17" wide by 9½" high.

Golf Clubs Clock

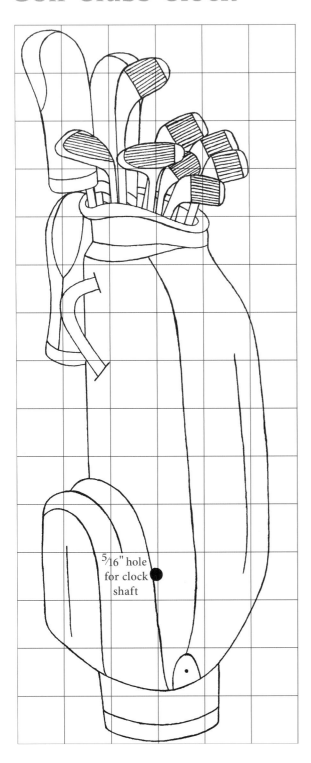

⁵⁄16" hole
for clock
shaft

Painting and Finishing

1. Stain and seal whole surface. Shadow with brown velvet and highlight with palomino tan.
2. Put a brown velvet wash on the clubs and on the upper base of the bag. Paint the lower base black, and paint the spaces between the clubs above the bag black as shown.
3. Paint the covers Wedgwood blue. Trim with nightfall blue. Shadow with Cape Cod blue and highlight with blue mist.
4. Spray with a clear high-gloss acrylic finish.
5. Attach a sawtooth hanger on back. Assemble clock movement, numbers, and hands on the finished piece.

Copy pattern at 230%. Finished size: about 5¾" wide by 17½" high.

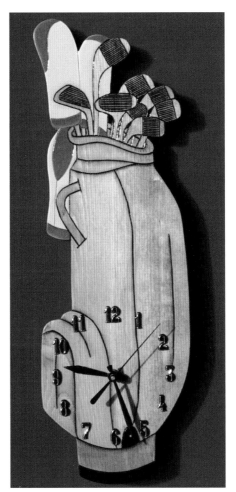

Tennis Racquet and Ball Clock

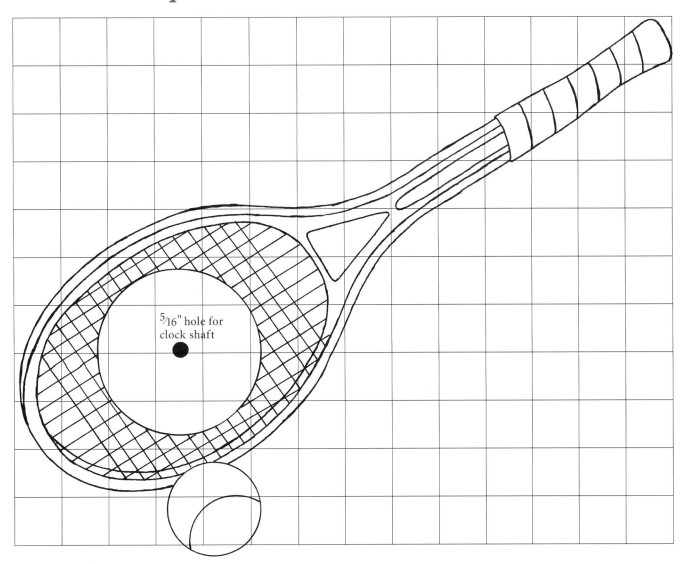

5/16" hole for clock shaft

Painting and Finishing

1. Stain and seal whole surface. Shadow with brown velvet and highlight with palomino tan.
2. Paint the handle black. Highlight with lichen grey.
3. Paint the ball in tide pool blue. Shadow with midnight blue. Highlight with blue heaven (medium blue).
4. Spray with a clear high-gloss acrylic finish.
5. Attach a sawtooth hanger on back. Assemble clock movement, numbers, and hands on the finished piece.

Copy pattern at 200%. Finished size: about 16" wide by 7" high.

Hot-Air Balloon Clock

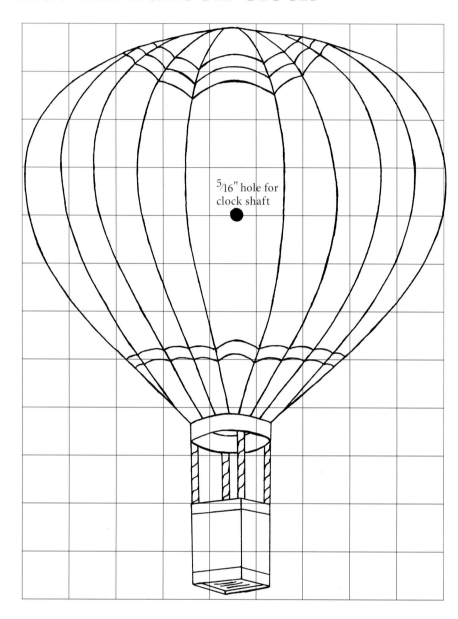

$^5/_{16}$" hole for clock shaft

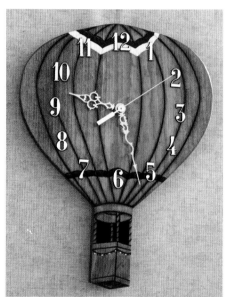

Painting and Finishing

1. Stain and seal whole surface. Shadow with brown velvet and highlight with palomino tan.
2. Paint stripes on the balloon red, white, and navy blue. Shadow red with maroon and highlight with antique white. Shadow white with antique white. For the blue stripe, shadow with midnight blue. Highlight with Wedgwood blue. Put red, white, and blue dots on box for decoration.
3. Paint the spaces between the ropes black.
4. Spray with a clear high-gloss acrylic finish.
5. Attach a sawtooth hanger on back. Assemble clock movement, numbers, and hands on the finished piece.

Copy pattern at 230%. Finished size: about 10½" wide by 14" tall.

Snowmobile Clock

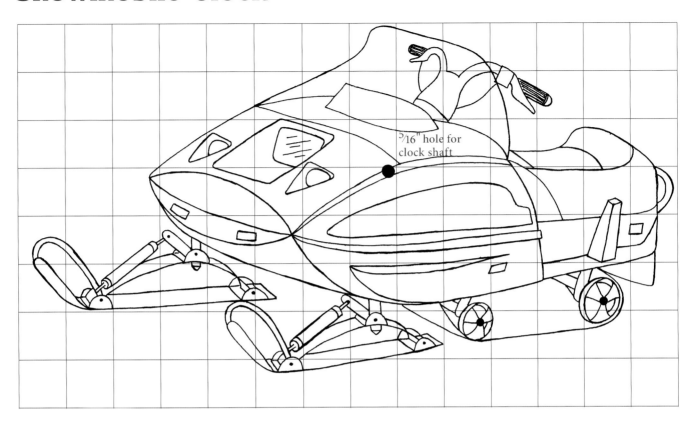

"5/16" hole for clock shaft

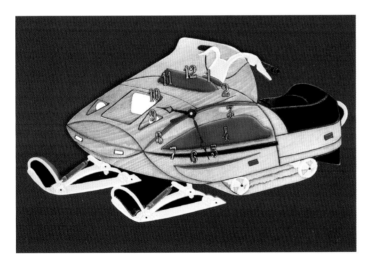

Painting and Finishing

1. Stain and seal whole surface.
2. Paint steering column, handlebars, handle at rear of the machine, wheels, and skis lichen grey. Highlight with white and shadow with hippo grey.
3. Paint reflectors on side of machine tomato spice (bright red). Paint lights yellow and highlight with white.
4. Paint bottom end of steering column, instrument panel, side panel of machine, and shocks Cape Cod blue. Shadow with midnight blue and highlight with blue mist.
5. Paint handlebar grips, flap at the rear of the machine, seat, and spaces around skis black. Highlight with lichen grey. Put black dots for axles of the wheels and for screw heads on the skis.
6. Spray with a clear high-gloss acrylic finish.
7. Attach a sawtooth hanger on back. Assemble clock movement, numbers, and hands on the finished piece.

Copy pattern at 235%. Finished size: about 16" wide by 8½" tall.

Airplane on Cloud Clock

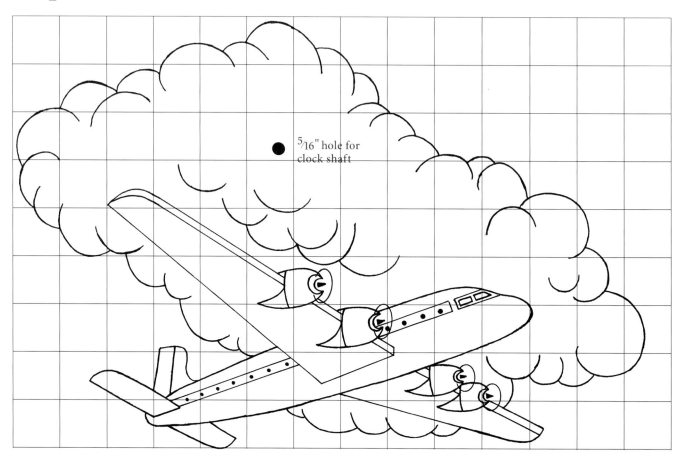

$^5/16$" hole for clock shaft

Painting and Finishing

1. Stain and seal whole surface.
2. Paint front part of engines, forward part of the tail, and edge of wings navy blue. Paint back part of engines and trim around windows lichen grey.
3. Highlight the rest of the plane and engines with lichen grey.
4. Paint silver on the windows.
5. With a flat brush, side-load with Quaker grey and paint inside of circles around front of engines.
6. Side-load a #12 flat brush with Quaker grey and paint clouds.
7. Spray with a clear high-gloss acrylic finish.
8. Attach a sawtooth hanger on back. Assemble clock movement, numbers, and hands on the finished piece.

Copy pattern at 240%. Finished size: about 16" wide by 10¾" tall.

Train Clock

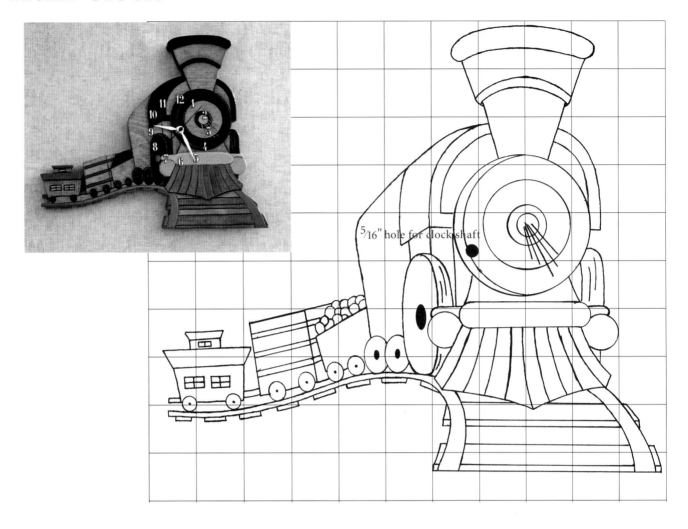

5/16" hole for clock shaft

Painting and Finishing

1. Stain and seal whole surface. Shadow with brown velvet. Highlight with palomino tan.

2. Paint top of smokestack, middle ring around stack, top section of engine, large and small ring around light, coal, and wheels black (see photo). Highlight with lichen grey and shadow with hippo grey. Paint the tracks and axles of wheels hippo grey. Highlight with lichen grey.

3. Paint the bar across the front of the engine lichen grey and highlight with white. Paint the balls just under the bar gold.

4. Put a brown velvet wash on the lower front of train and highlight with palomino tan. Put a burnt umber wash on the ties.

5. Paint red on the top of the caboose and on the stripes on the box car.

6. With straw, paint the light on the front of the engine and the windows on the caboose. Pull lines with straw for the light rays.

7. Spray with a clear high-gloss acrylic finish.

8. Attach a sawtooth hanger on back. Assemble clock movement, numbers, and hands on the finished piece.

Copy pattern at 230%. Finished size: about 12¼" wide by 11" tall.

Motorcycle Clock

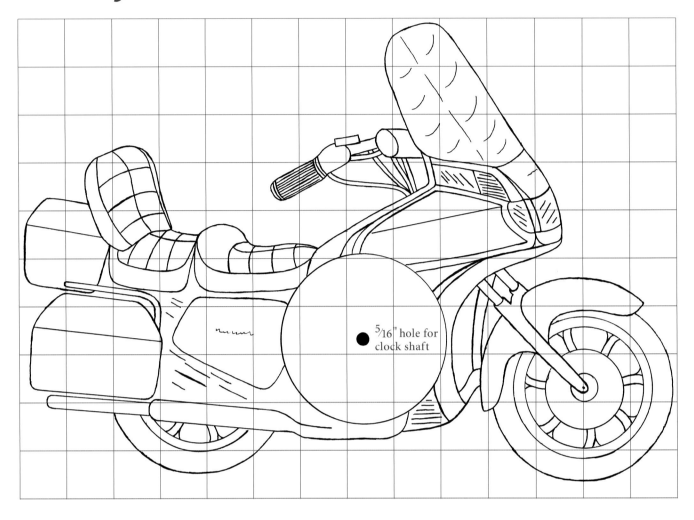

5/16" hole for clock shaft

Painting and Finishing

1. Stain and seal whole surface.
2. Paint spokes, pipes, and handlebars lichen grey. Highlight with white. Shadow with hippo grey.
3. Paint the tires, seats, and handlebar grips black. Highlight with lichen grey.
4. Paint faring, fender, and carriers candy bar brown. Highlight with Indiana rose.
5. Paint lights yellow and highlight with white.
6. Spray with a clear high-gloss acrylic finish.
7. Attach a sawtooth hanger on back. Assemble clock movement, numbers, and hands on the finished piece.

Copy pattern at 230%. Finished size: about 16" wide by 11" tall.

Truck Clock or Coat Rack

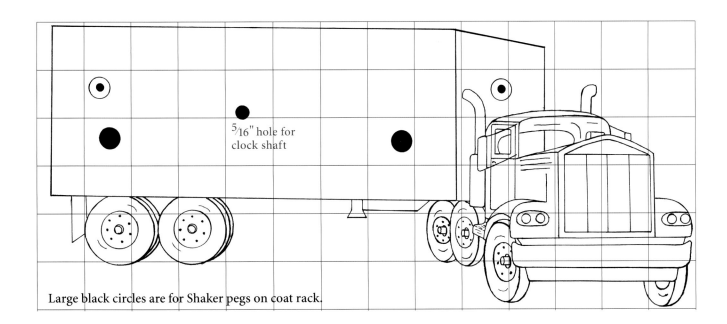

5/16" hole for clock shaft

Large black circles are for Shaker pegs on coat rack.

Painting and Finishing the Clock

1. Stain and seal whole surface. Shadow with brown velvet and highlight with palomino tan.
2. Paint the tires black and highlight with lichen grey.
3. Paint the rims, smokestacks, grille, step, around the lights, and bumper lichen grey. Highlight with white and shadow with hippo grey. Paint the lights straw.
4. Paint name of company with black lettering for the clock; or paint child's name for the coat rack.
5. Spray with a clear high-gloss acrylic finish.
6. Attach a sawtooth hanger on back. Assemble clock movement, numbers, and hands on the finished piece.

To Make, Paint, and Finish the Coat Rack

Additional supplies for coat rack:

- Two 1½" screws
- Two ½" round screw hole plugs
- Two 3½" Shaker pegs

1. Drill two ½" wide holes, ⅝" deep, for the Shaker pegs (large black circles). Drill two ¼" wide holes through as marked on the pattern (white circles) for wall mounting. With a ½" Forstner bit, drill over the top of these two holes about ¼" deep so the plugs will fit in and cover the screw heads.
2. Stain, seal, and paint the same as for the truck clock. Stain the Shaker pegs and screw hole plugs.
3. Install the 3½" Shaker pegs before spraying the rack with a clear high-gloss acrylic finish. Spray the ½" round top screw hole plugs separately.

Copy pattern at 220%. Finished size: about 15" wide by 6½" tall.

Boat Clock

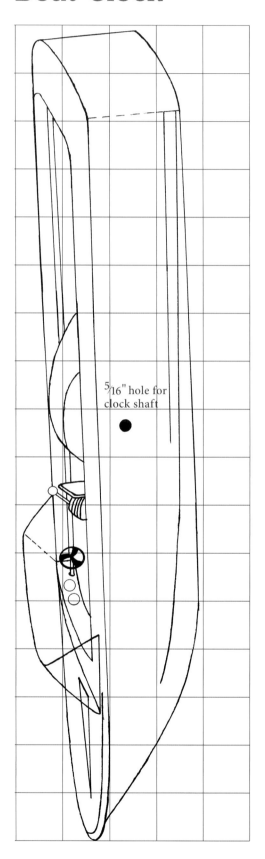

5/16" hole for clock shaft

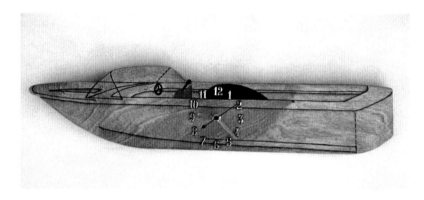

Painting and Finishing

1. Stain and seal whole surface. Shadow with brown velvet and highlight with palomino tan.
2. Paint the steering wheel, throttle, and engine cover black. Highlight with lichen grey.
3. Paint the steering column lichen grey and line the speedometer and tachometer with lichen grey.
4. Paint the seat tomato spice and highlight with Indiana rose.
5. Spray with a clear high-gloss acrylic finish.
6. Attach 2 sawtooth hangers on back. Assemble clock movement, numbers, and hands on the finished piece.

Copy pattern at 245%. Finished size: about 21" wide by 4½" tall.

Anchor Clock

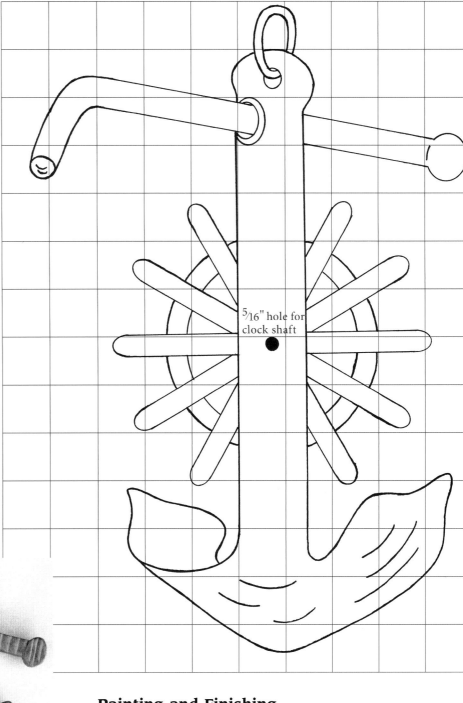

⁵/16" hole for clock shaft

Copy pattern at 225%.
Finished size: about
10½" wide by 15" tall.

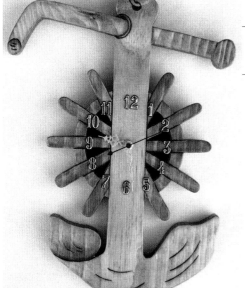

Painting and Finishing

1. Stain and seal whole surface. Shadow with brown velvet. Highlight with palomino tan.
2. Put a burnt umber wash on the ship wheel. Paint spaces inside the spokes and the chain loop black.
3. Spray with a clear high-gloss acrylic finish.
4. Attach a sawtooth hanger on back. Assemble clock movement, numbers, and hands on the finished piece.

Music Staff (Treble and Base Clef) Clock

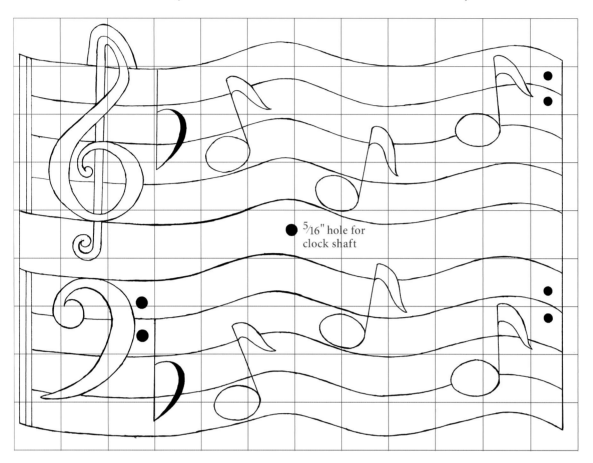

● ⁵/16" hole for clock shaft

Painting and Finishing the Clock

1. Stain and seal whole surface.
2. Paint the notes, clefs, flats, and dots black.
3. Spray with a clear high-gloss acrylic finish.
4. Attach a sawtooth hanger on back.
5. Assemble clock movement, numbers, and hands on the finished staff piece.

Copy pattern at 250%. Finished size: about 14½" wide by 11" high.

Music Staff (Treble Clef) Clock or Mug Holder

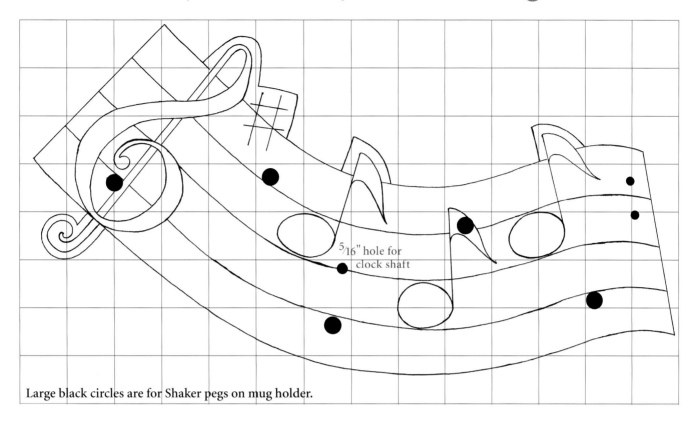

⁵⁄₁₆" hole for clock shaft

Large black circles are for Shaker pegs on mug holder.

Copy pattern at 280%. Finished size: about 19" wide by 9" high.

Painting and Finishing the Clock

1. Stain and seal whole surface.
2. Paint the notes, dots, and clef black.
3. Spray with a clear high-gloss acrylic finish.
4. Attach a sawtooth hanger on back. Assemble clock movement, numbers, and hands on the finished staff piece.

Painting and Finishing the Mug Holder

Additional supplies needed for mug holder: Five 3½" mug pegs. The mug holder pictured is made from ¾" birch plywood, stained with American walnut.

1. Do not drill the clock hole.
2. Drill five ½" wide holes, ⅝" deep, for the mug pegs (large black circles on pattern).
3. Stain, seal, and paint the same as for the clock. Stain the mug pegs.
4. Install the mug pegs and spray with a clear high-gloss acrylic finish.
5. Attach two sawtooth hangers on the back.

Grand Piano Clock

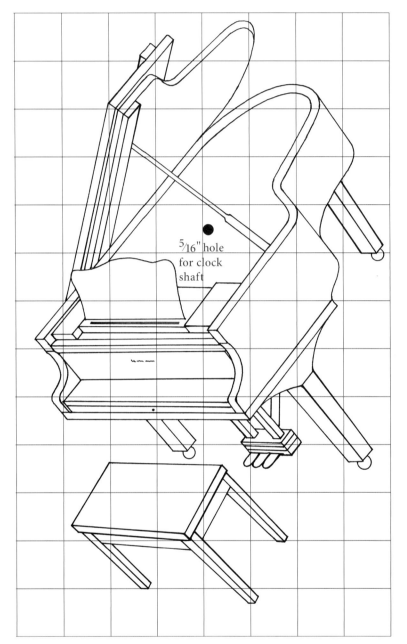

$^5/_{16}$" hole for clock shaft

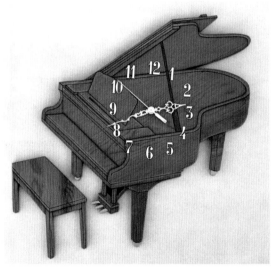

Painting and Finishing

1. Stain and seal whole surface. Shadow with brown velvet and highlight with palomino tan.
2. Put a brown velvet wash on the rod that holds the piano top up.
3. Paint the pedals and wheels gold. Put a gold dot below the keyboard cover for keyhole.
4. Paint black in the space between the braces that hold the pedals.
5. Spray with a clear high-gloss acrylic finish.
6. Attach a sawtooth hanger on back.
7. Assemble clock movement, numbers, and hands on the finished piece.

Copy pattern at 280%. Finished size of the piano is about 12" wide by 14" high. Bench is 4½" wide by 6¼" high.

Baby Grand Piano Clock

Painting and Finishing

1. Stain and seal whole surface. Shadow with brown velvet and highlight with palomino tan.
2. Put a brown velvet wash on the rod that holds the top up.
3. Paint the pedals and wheels gold. Put a gold dot below the keyboard cover for keyhole.
4. Paint black in the space between the arms that hold the pedals.
5. Spray with a clear high-gloss acrylic finish.
6. Attach a sawtooth hanger on back. Assemble clock movement, numbers, and hands on the finished piece.

Copy pattern at 300%. Finished size: about 11¼" wide by 13½" high.

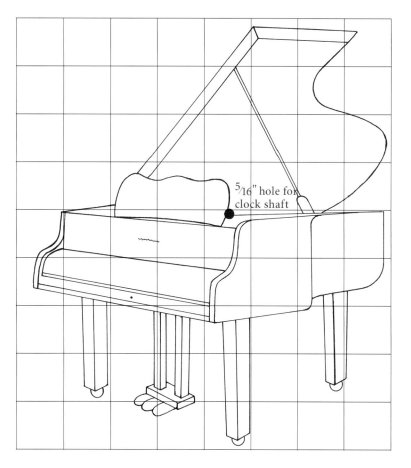

5⁄16" hole for clock shaft

Violin Clock

straight grain of wood

⁵⁄₁₆" hole for
clock shaft

Additional supplies: 4 tie pegs

Painting and Finishing

1. Drill two ³⁄₁₆" wide holes, ¼" deep, on each side of the neck for violin pegs, at lines marked on pattern. Saw the pegs so they are ½" long.
2. Stain and seal whole surface. Shadow with brown velvet and highlight with palomino tan.
3. Paint the pad black and highlight with lichen grey.
4. Spray with a clear high-gloss acrylic finish.
5. Attach a sawtooth hanger on back. Assemble clock movement, numbers, and hands on the finished piece.

Copy pattern at 250%. Finished size: about 5¼" wide by 15⅝" long.

Guitar Clock

Additional supplies: Six ⅜" wide round-head screw-hole plugs

Preparing, Painting, and Finishing

1. Mark and drill six ⅜" wide holes, ⅛" deep, in the upper end (head) of the guitar piece for the ⅜" round-head screw-hole plugs.
2. Trace detailed pattern onto the wood piece and detail with a wood-burning tool. Sand again with 320-grit sandpaper to remove trace marks, sap, and ashes. Insert the ⅜" round-head screw-hole plugs and glue in place.
3. Stain and seal the whole surface. Shadow with brown velvet and highlight with palomino tan.
4. Spray with a clear high-gloss acrylic finish.
5. Attach a sawtooth hanger on back. Assemble clock movement, numbers, and hands on the finished piece.

Copy pattern at 240%. Finished size: about 6½" wide by 16½" high.

⁵⁄₁₆" hole for clock shaft

Treble Clef and Notes Clock or Wall Hanging

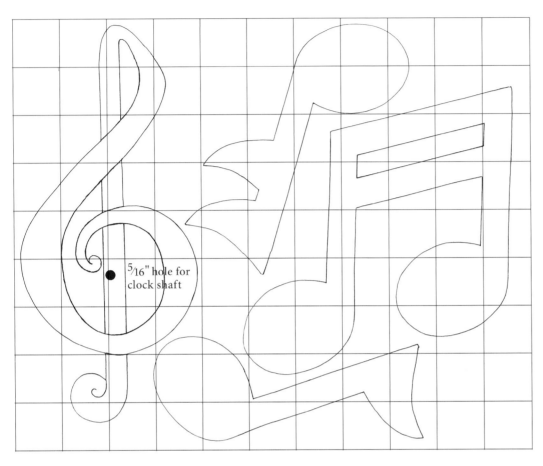

⁵/16" hole for clock shaft

Copy pattern at 300%. Approximate treble clef finished size is 5¾" wide by 12½" high.

Painting and Finishing Both

1. Stain and seal whole surface.
2. Paint treble clef and notes black. Highlight with lichen grey (see photo).
3. Spray with a clear high-gloss acrylic finish.
4. Attach sawtooth hangers on the backs.

For the Clock

Assemble clock movement, numbers, and hands on the finished treble clef piece.

For the Wall Hanging

For wall hanging without clock, do not rout the 3" clock hole or drill the ⁵/16" hole in the treble clef.

Scissors and Thread Clock

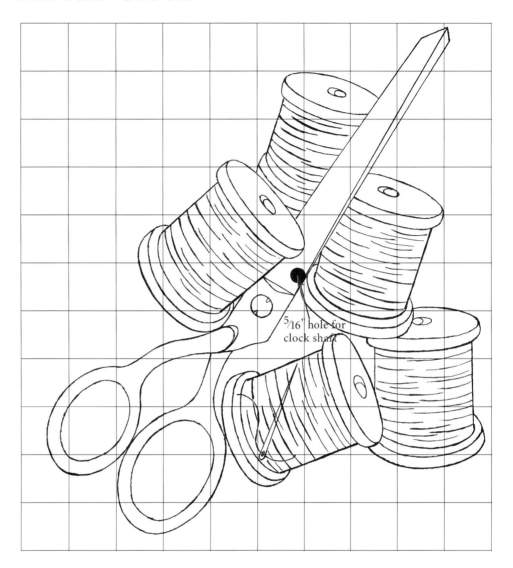

5/16" hole for clock shaft

Copy pattern at 200%.
Finished size: about 9½"
wide by 10½" tall.

Painting and Finishing

1. Stain and seal whole surface. Shadow the spools with brown velvet and highlight with palomino tan.
2. Paint the scissors and needle lichen grey. Shadow with hippo grey and highlight with white. Paint the spaces in the scissors and between the spools of thread and scissors black, or whatever color you like.
3. Paint the spools of thread tomato spice, yellow, Seminole green, Wedgwood blue, and Indiana rose. With the liner brush, pull lines to bring out the thread. Use maroon on the tomato spice; straw on the yellow; dark jungle green on the Seminole green; Cape Cod blue on the Wedgwood blue; and white on the Indiana rose.
4. Spray with a clear high-gloss acrylic finish.
5. Attach a sawtooth hanger on back. Assemble clock movement, numbers, and hands on the finished piece.

Tooth Clock

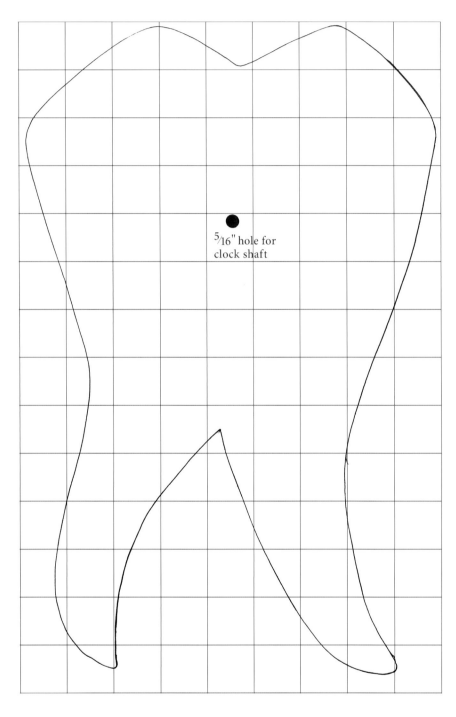

$^{5}/_{16}$" hole for
clock shaft

Copy pattern at 220%.
Finished size: about 9⅝"
wide by 15" tall.

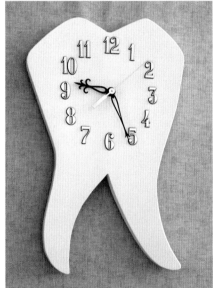

Painting and Finishing

1. Stain back side and seal both sides.
2. Paint several coats of white and finish off by
   daubing on white, using an old frayed brush.
3. Spray with a clear high-gloss acrylic finish.
4. Attach a sawtooth hanger on back. Assemble clock
   movement, numbers, and hands on the finished piece.

Heart with Arrow Clock

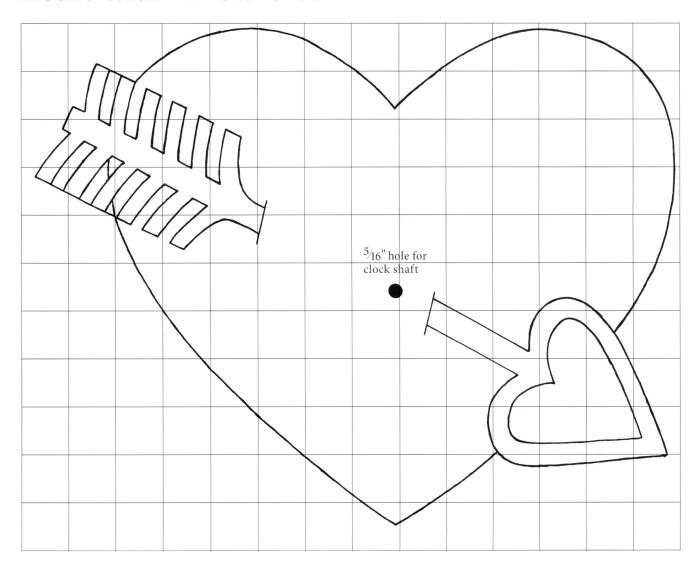

$^5/16$" hole for clock shaft

Painting and Finishing

1. Stain and seal whole surface.
2. Paint the arrow burgundy rose. Paint the center of the heart on the arrow Indiana rose. Shadow the Indiana rose with burgundy rose. Put gold dots around the edge of the arrow.
3. Paint Indiana rose and burgundy border around edge of heart. Paint the "I Love You" lettering with black.
4. Spray with a clear high-gloss acrylic finish.
5. Attach a sawtooth hanger on back. Assemble clock movement, numbers, and hands on the finished piece.

Copy pattern at 215%. Finished size: about 14½" wide by 10¾" tall.

Balanced Scales Clock

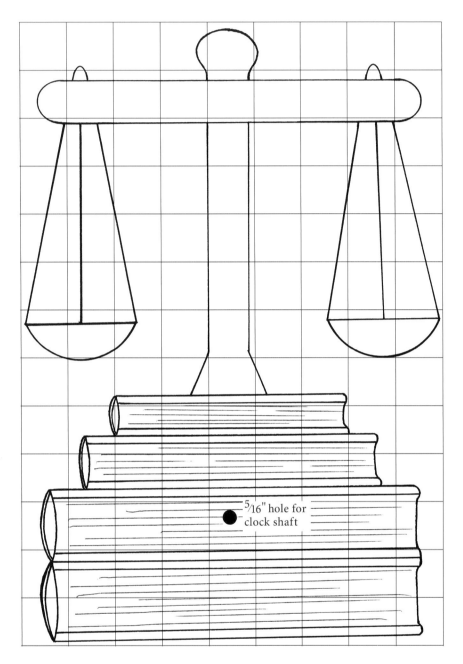

5/16" hole for clock shaft

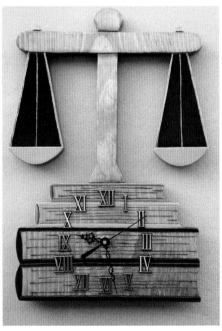

Painting and Finishing

1. Stain and seal whole surface. Shadow with brown velvet. Highlight with palomino tan.
2. Paint the cover of the top book Seminole green. Use Wedgwood blue on the second book cover. Use burnt umber on the third book cover and midnight blue on the bottom book cover.
3. Paint black between the rods holding the pans. Paint the pans and rods gold.
4. Spray with a clear high-gloss acrylic finish.
5. Attach a sawtooth hanger on back. Assemble clock movement, roman numerals, and hands on the finished piece.

Copy pattern at 215%. Finished size: about 9½" wide by 13½" tall.

Computer Clock

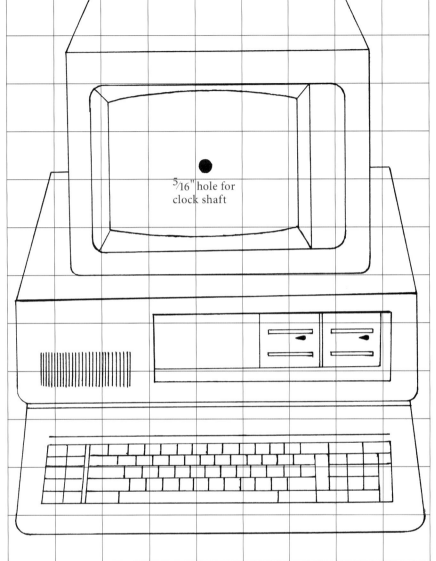

5/16" hole for clock shaft

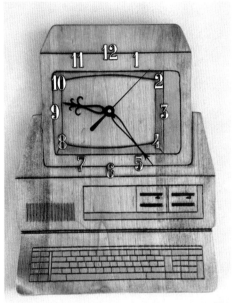

Painting and Finishing

1. Shadow with brown velvet and highlight with palomino tan.
2. Spray with a clear high-gloss acrylic finish.
3. Attach a sawtooth hanger on back. Assemble clock movement, numbers, and hands on the finished piece.

Copy pattern at 220%. Finished size: about 9½" wide by 12½" tall.

Cards Clock

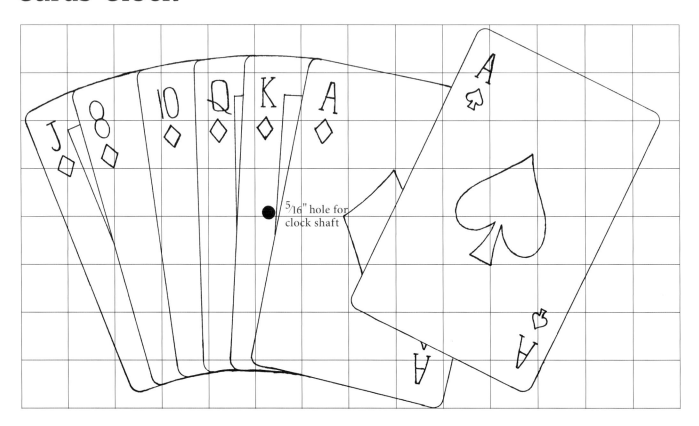

5/16" hole for clock shaft

Painting and Finishing

1. Stain and seal whole surface. Shadow with brown velvet and highlight with palomino tan.
2. Paint the diamonds in tomato spice (bright red). Paint the spades black.
3. Spray with a clear high-gloss acrylic finish.
4. Attach a sawtooth hanger on back. Assemble clock movement, numbers, and hands on the finished piece.

Copy pattern at 220%. Finished size: about 15" wide by 9" tall.

Carpenter's Tools Clock

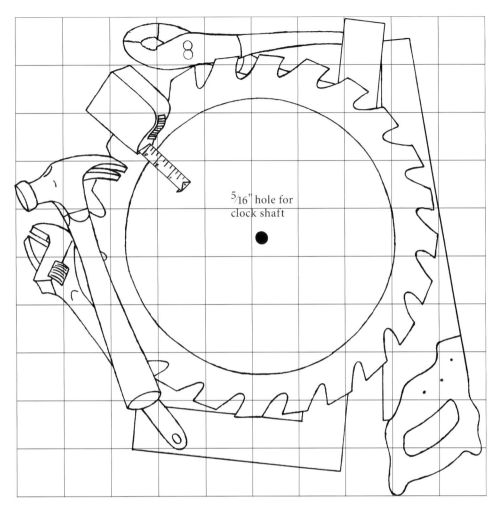

$^5/16$" hole for
clock shaft

Copy pattern at 235%.
Finished size: about
11½" wide by 11¾" tall.

Painting and Finishing

1. Stain and seal whole surface. Shadow with brown velvet. Highlight with palomino tan.
2. Paint hammer head, crescent wrench, pliers head, tape measure tape, and handsaw blade lichen grey. Shadow with hippo grey and highlight with antique white.
3. Paint tape measure case straw. Highlight with antique white.
4. Paint pliers handles tomato spice. Highlight with Indiana rose.
5. Paint hammer handle and hand saw handle brown velvet. Highlight with palomino tan and shadow with burnt umber. Use palomino tan for the dots on the saw handle.
6. Paint the release button on the tape measure, the spaces between tools, the space in the saw handle, and between pliers parts black.
7. Spray with a clear high-gloss acrylic finish.
8. Attach a sawtooth hanger on back. Assemble clock movement, numbers, and hands on the finished piece.

Praying Hands Clock

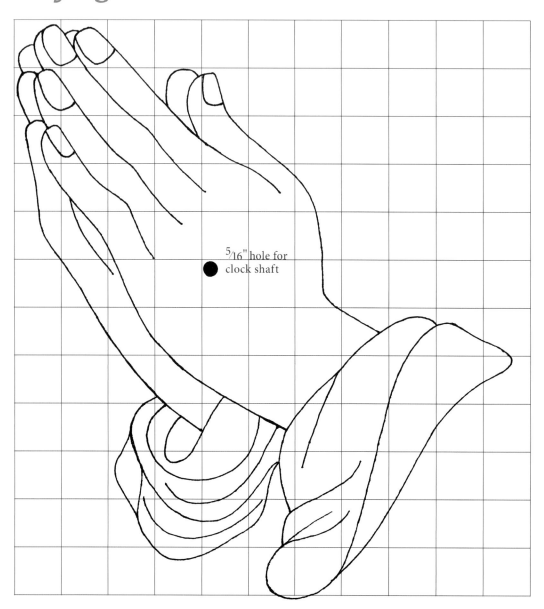

5/16" hole for clock shaft

Painting and Finishing

1. Stain with Puritan pine and seal whole surface. Shadow with brown velvet and highlight with palomino tan.
2. Put a light flesh tan wash on fingernails.
3. Paint the cuffs antique white. Shadow with flesh tan and highlight with white.
4. Spray with a clear high-gloss acrylic finish.
5. Attach a sawtooth hanger on back. Assemble clock movement, numbers, and hands on the finished piece.

Copy pattern at 150%. Finished size: about 8" wide by 12" tall.

Open Book Clock

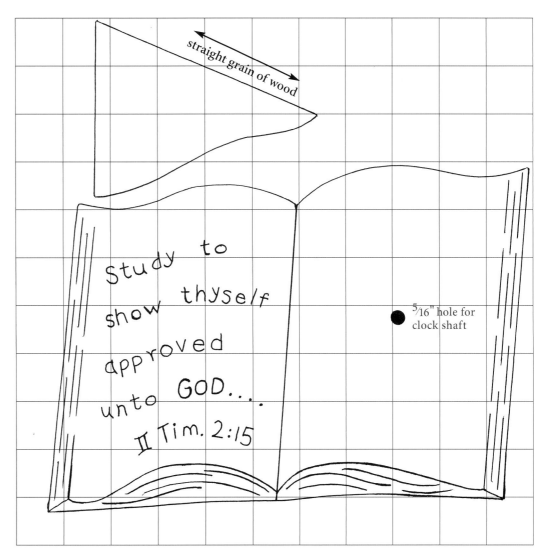

straight grain of wood

Study to show thyself approved unto GOD.... II Tim. 2:15

⁵⁄16" hole for clock shaft

Painting and Finishing

Cut out the stand if you want a desk clock; its not needed for the wall clock. Additional supplies (optional): open-book clock dial.

1. Stain and seal whole surface. Shadow with brown velvet. Highlight with palomino tan.
2. Put a palomino tan wash on the edges of the pages. Trace verse on the open book and paint the lettering with black.
3. Spray with a clear high-gloss acrylic finish.
4. Attach the stand in center of the back with carpenter's glue and secure with small finish nails for a desk clock, or attach a sawtooth hanger for a wall clock. Assemble the clock movement. Attach an open book clock dial (optional) or standard numbers, and add the hands on the finished piece.

Copy pattern at 195%. Finished size: about 10" wide by 7" tall.

Potty Clock

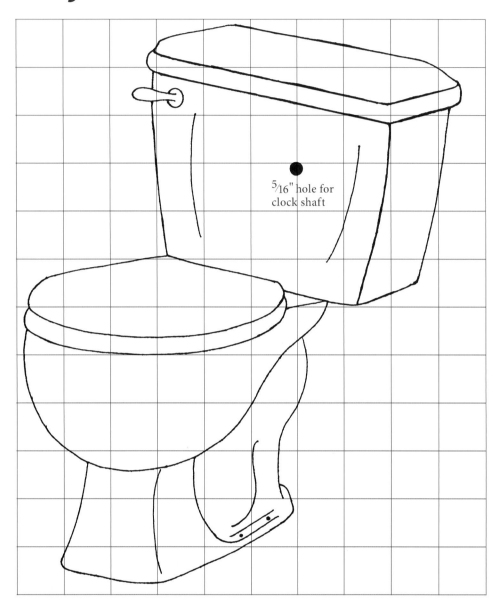

5/16" hole for clock shaft

Painting and Finishing

1. Stain and seal whole surface. Shadow with brown velvet. Shadow with palomino tan.
2. To paint each flower on the toilet lid, paint 6 white commas in a circle. Put a straw dot in the flower center. With Seminole green, pull stems and sprays. Put white dots along the top third of the sprays. Paint green commas along the stems for leaves.
3. Spray with a clear high-gloss acrylic finish.
4. Attach a sawtooth hanger on back. Assemble clock movement, numbers, and hands on the finished piece.

Copy pattern at 220%. Finished size: about 10½" wide by 13" tall.

Unicorn on Heart Clock or Necklace Holder

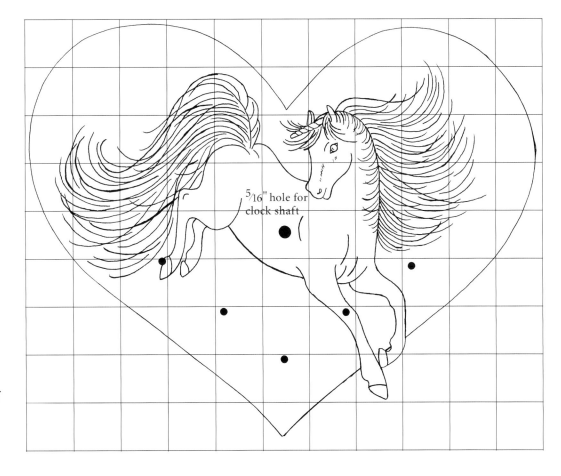

⁵⁄16" hole for clock shaft

Copy pattern at 255%. Finished size: about 13½" wide by 10¾" tall. Small circles are for tie pegs of necklace holder.

Painting and Finishing the Clock

1. Stain and seal whole surface. Shadow with brown velvet and highlight with palomino tan.
2. Dry-brush with white through the mane and tail. Using antique white and a liner brush, pull through all the lines of the mane and tail. Paint the hooves antique white. Highlight with white.
3. Paint the eye and nostril black. Paint tiny white commas on the eye.
4. Paint a border of commas and dots around edge of heart with Indiana rose and white.
5. Spray with a clear high-gloss acrylic finish.
6. Attach a sawtooth hanger on back. Assemble clock movement, numbers, and hands on the finished piece.

Painting and Finishing the Necklace Holder

Additional supplies for necklace holder: 5 tie pegs

1. Drill five ³⁄16" wide holes, ⅝" deep, for the tie pegs, as shown on the pattern by small black dots.
2. Stain, seal and paint the same as for the clock.
3. Install the five tie pegs; then spray with a clear high-gloss acrylic finish. Attach 2 sawtooth hangers on back.

Rosebud in Vase Clock

5/16" hole for clock shaft

Painting and Finishing

1. Stain and seal whole surface. Shadow the vase with brown velvet and highlight with palomino tan.
2. Paint the rose in Indiana rose. Shadow with gypsy rose and highlight with white.
3. Paint the stem and leaves Seminole green. Double-load a flat brush with dark jungle green and Seminole green and paint over the leaves on the shadow side. Double-load with Seminole and apple green and paint over the leaves on the upper side (highlight side). Paint the spaces between the leaf and stem, and between leaf and flower, black.
4. Spray with a clear high-gloss acrylic finish.
5. Attach a sawtooth hanger to the back. Assemble clock movement, numbers, and hands on the finished piece.

Copy pattern at 230%. Finished size: about 6¼" wide by 15¼" high.

Three Rosebuds in Vase Clock

Painting and Finishing

1. Stain the back and seal both sides.

2. Paint a coat of gesso over the front and edges.

3. Paint the rosebuds Indiana Rose. Shadow with gypsy rose and highlight with white. Paint the stem and leaves Seminole green.

4. Double-load a flat brush with dark jungle green and Seminole green and paint over the leaves on the shadow sides. Double-load with Seminole green and apple green and paint over the leaves on the upper half to highlight. Paint the spaces between the rosebuds, and between the buds and leaves, black.

5. Paint the vase antique white. Shadow with maple sugar and highlight with white.

6. Spray with a clear high-gloss acrylic finish.

7. Attach a sawtooth hanger to the back. Assemble clock movement, numbers, and hands on the finished piece.

5/16" hole for clock shaft

Copy pattern at 200%. Finished size: about 5" wide by 16" high.

Rose Flower Clock

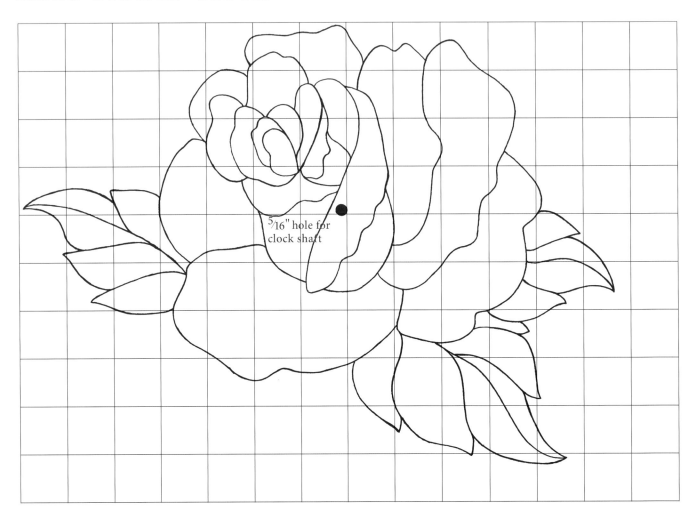

5/16" hole for clock shaft

Painting and Finishing

1. Stain the back and seal both sides.
2. Paint the rose with Indiana rose. Shadow with gypsy rose and highlight with white.
3. Paint the leaves Seminole green. Double-load a flat brush with dark jungle green and Seminole green and paint over the leaves on the shadow side. Double-load with Seminole and apple green and paint over the leaves on the upper half to highlight.
4. Spray with a clear high-gloss acrylic finish.
5. Attach a sawtooth hanger to the back. Assemble clock movement, numbers, and hands on the finished piece.

Copy pattern at 250%. Finished size: about 16" wide by 11½" high.

Teddy Bear with Heart Clock

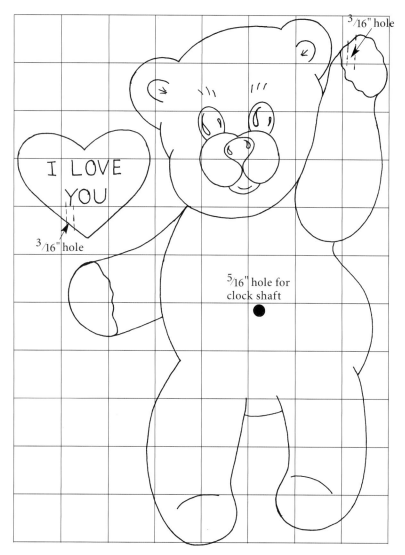

Additional supplies for this project:
- ¼" wide wood dowel, 6" long
- wood glue

Painting and Finishing

1. Drill holes ¾" deep for a ¼" wide, 6" long dowel in the top of the teddy bear's paw and in the heart, as shown on the pattern.
2. Stain and seal whole surface. Shadow with brown velvet. Highlight with palomino tan.
3. Daub muzzle and inside of ears with maple sugar. Float adobe underneath eyes on muzzle and on tongue. Highlight with tiny white commas. Pull adobe lines in the ears.
4. Paint eyes and nose black. Paint white upside-down commas on left side of eyes and a small comma on the right side. Paint white upside-down commas on the nose for nostrils. Highlight muzzle around mouth with white.
5. Paint lettering on heart black. Paint small coma-dot border around edge of heart with red and maple sugar tan.
6. Glue in the dowel with wood glue. Spray with a clear high-gloss acrylic finish.
7. Attach a sawtooth hanger on back. Assemble clock movement, numbers, and hands on the finished piece.

   Copy pattern at 250%. Finished teddy bear size is about 8½" wide by 13" tall.

Teddy Bear with Bow Clock

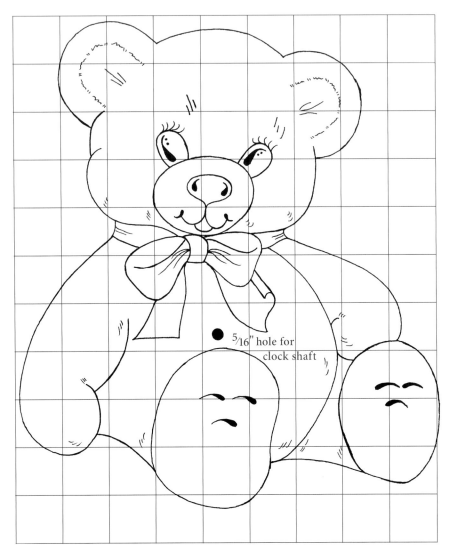

⬤ 5/16" hole for clock shaft

Painting and Finishing

1. Stain and seal whole surface. Shadow with brown velvet. Highlight with palomino tan.
2. With an old frayed brush, daub muzzle, inside of ears, and middle of the bottoms of the feet with maple sugar. Float adobe underneath eyes on muzzle and on tongue. Highlight with tiny white commas. Pull adobe lines in the ears.
3. Paint eyes and nose black. Paint white upside-down commas on left side of eyes and a small comma on the right side. Paint white upside-down commas on the nose for nostrils. Highlight muzzle around mouth with white. Paint black eyelashes. Paint a small black comma at each end of the mouth. Paint black commas on the bottom of the feet and float adobe underneath the commas.
4. Paint the bow Wedgwood blue. Shadow with Cape Cod blue and highlight with blue mist. Paint a gold comma on each end of the ribbon and gold commas on the knot.
5. Spray with a clear high-gloss acrylic finish.
6. Attach a sawtooth hanger on back. Assemble clock movement, numbers, and hands on the finished piece.

Copy pattern at 240%. Finished size: about 11" wide by 12½" tall.

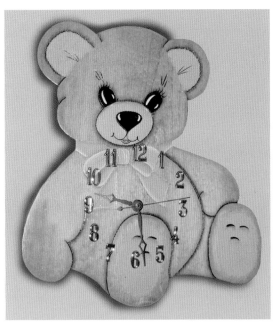

Cuddly Teddy Bear Clock

Painting and Finishing

1. Stain and seal whole surface. Shadow with brown velvet. Highlight with palomino tan.

2. Daub muzzle and inside of ears with maple sugar tan. Float adobe underneath eyes on muzzle and on tongue. Highlight with tiny white commas. Pull adobe lines in the ears.

3. Paint eyes and nose black. Paint eyelashes black. Paint white upside-down commas on left side of eyes and a small comma on the right side. Paint white upside-down commas on the nose for nostrils. Highlight muzzle around mouth with white.

4. Paint the space between the legs black.

5. Spray with a clear high-gloss acrylic finish.

6. Attach a sawtooth hanger on back. Assemble clock movement, numbers, and hands on the finished piece.

Copy pattern at 265%. Finished size: about 11¼" wide by 14½" tall.

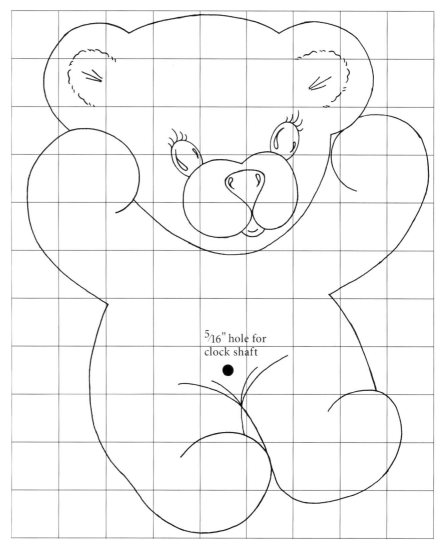

⁵⁄16" hole for clock shaft

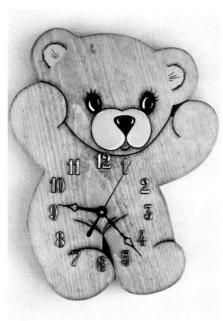

Baby Bear Profile Clock or Coat Rack

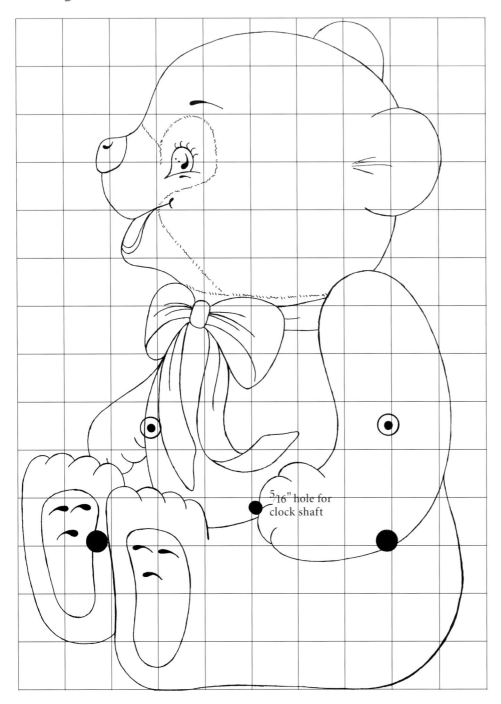

⁵⁄₁₆" hole for clock shaft

Copy pattern at 220%. Finished teddy bear size: about 10½" wide by 15½" tall. Large black circles are for pegs on coat rack. White circles are for coat rack wall mounting.

Painting and Finishing the Clock

1. Stain and seal whole surface. Shadow with brown velvet. Highlight with palomino tan.

2. With an old frayed brush, daub muzzle and around eye, under mouth, inside of ear, and middle of the bottoms of the feet with maple sugar tan. Float adobe underneath eye on muzzle and on tongue. Highlight with tiny white commas. Pull adobe lines in the ear.

3. Paint eyes and nose black. Paint white upside-down comma on right side of eye and a small comma on the left side. Paint white upside-down comma on the nose for nostril. Highlight muzzle around mouth and nose with white. Paint black eyelashes and brow. Paint a small black comma at the end of the mouth. Paint black commas on the bottom of the feet and float adobe underneath the commas.

4. Paint the bow Indiana rose. Shadow with gypsy rose and highlight with white. Paint a gold comma on each end of the ribbon and gold commas on the knot.

5. Paint the space between the body and feet black.

6. Spray with a clear high-gloss acrylic finish.

7. Attach a sawtooth hanger on back. Assemble clock movement, numbers, and hands on the finished piece.

Painting and Finishing Coat Rack

Additional supplies for coat rack:

• Two 1½" screws
• Two ½" wide round-top screw hole plugs
• Two 3½" long Shaker pegs

1. Stain, seal and paint as for the clock. Stain Shaker pegs and screw hole plugs.

2. Drill two ½" wide holes, ⅝" deep, for the Shaker pegs at the large black dots on the pattern. Drill two ¼" wide holes through wood at the white circles on pattern, for wall mounting. With a ½" Forstner bit, drill over the top of these two holes approximately ¼" deep so the plugs will fit in and cover the screw heads, but don't insert them yet.

3. Insert the 3½" long Shaker pegs; then spray with a clear high-gloss acrylic finish. Spray the ½" round-top screw plugs separately. Insert the plugs over the screws after the coat rack is mounted on the wall.

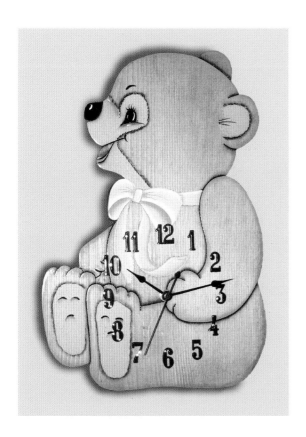

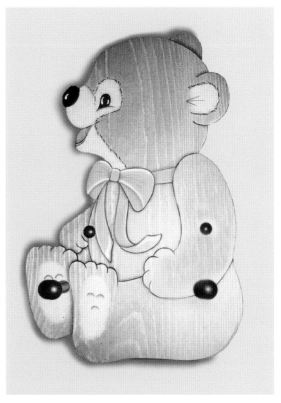

Carousel Clock or Welcome Sign

drill ⁵⁄₁₆" hole

⁵⁄₁₆" hole for clock shaft

WELCOME

Copy pattern at 310%.
Finished size: about 12½"
wide by 17" tall.

Additional supplies:

- ⁵⁄₁₆" wide wood dowel, 9" long
- One or two 1" hardwood balls
- Wood glue
- Thin white and light blue ribbons, 30" long

For Both

1. In the saddle area on the top edge, drill a vertical ⁵⁄₁₆" wide hole into the wood horse for the dowel; make the hole about 2" deep.

2. Also drill a ⁵⁄₁₆" wide hole into a 1" hardwood ball, about ½" deep, for the top of the dowel. (If you want two balls at the top, drill a ⁵⁄₁₆" wide hole through one hardwood ball and drill a similar hole about ½" deep into the other ball.)

3. Glue the 9" dowel into the hole in the top edge of the horse.

4. Glue the hardwood ball on the top end of the dowel. (If you are using two, slide the one that is drilled through ½" down on the dowel, and glue the other one on top.)

Painting Both

1. Stain and seal whole surface. Shadow with brown velvet and highlight with palomino tan.
2. Paint the eye black. Paint tiny white commas on the eye.
3. Paint mane, tail, and hooves antique white. Shadow with flesh tan and highlight with white.
4. Paint spaces between legs and body, between back legs and tail, and between the body and the drum black.
5. Paint the pole gold. Paint bridle, saddle, breast strap, and ball (for the pole) Wedgwood blue. Shadow with Cape Cod blue and highlight with blue mist.
6. Double-load a flat brush with nightfall blue and white to paint the flowers on the breast strap and behind the saddle. Double-load the flat brush with Seminole green and dark jungle green for the leaves and stems. Make little white flowers with white dots. Put straw dots in center of flowers.
7. Paint gold commas around edge of saddle and breast strap. Paint a few gold commas around the flowers. Paint the rings on the bridle gold. Put gold dots on the bridle.

To Finish the Clock

1. Spray with a clear high-gloss acrylic finish.
2. Attach a sawtooth hanger on back. Assemble clock movement, numbers, and hands on the finished piece.
3. With a white ribbon and a blue ribbon, tie a bow below the ball on the pole. (Tie between the balls if you are using two.)

To Finish the Welcome Sign

1. Paint "WELCOME" on the drum with black lettering.
2. Spray with a clear high-gloss acrylic finish.
3. Attach a sawtooth hanger on the back.
4. With a white ribbon and a blue ribbon, tie a bow below the ball on the pole. (Tie between the balls if you are using two.)

Carousel Horse Clock

drill ⁵⁄₁₆" hole

⁵⁄₁₆" hole for clock shaft

Copy pattern at 260%. Finished size is about 13½" wide by 11" high (not including pole).

Additional supplies:

- ⁵⁄₁₆" wood dowel, about 14" long
- Two 1" hardwood balls
- Wood glue
- Thin red, white, and black ribbons, about 20" long

Painting and Finishing

1. Drill a ⁵⁄₁₆" wide hole into two 1" hardwood balls, about ½" deep, for the ends of the dowel. Drill a ⁵⁄₁₆" hole through the horse from the top through to the belly (dashed line). Insert, center, and glue the dowel into the horse (see photo). Glue the hardwood balls on each end of the dowel.
2. Stain and seal whole surface. Shadow with brown velvet and highlight with palomino tan.
3. Paint eye black. Paint tiny white commas on the eye. Paint mane, tail, and hooves antique white. Shadow with flesh tan and highlight with white. Paint black in the spaces between front legs, back legs, and between body and tail black. Float adobe on the tongue. Highlight with a tiny white comma.
4. Paint the pole gold. Paint the bridle, saddle, balls (on each end of the dowel), and the bands the tassels are on tomato spice. Highlight with antique white. Paint the circle on the bridle and all the tassels gold. Put gold dots on the bridle.
5. Paint the blanket black and trim with tomato spice. Highlight the black with lichen grey. Put groups of 3 gold dots on the saddle.
6. Spray with a clear high-gloss acrylic finish.
7. Attach a sawtooth hanger on back. Assemble clock movement, numbers and hands on finished piece.
8. Using one black ribbon, one white ribbon, and one red ribbon, tie a bow under the top ball on the pole.

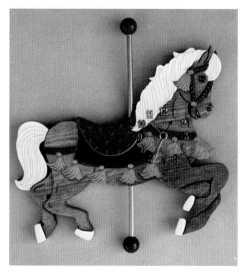

Patches the Clown Clock

Additional supplies: Three 24" lengths of narrow ribbon to match balloons. There are 2 separate patterns, the clown and the balloons. Cut each out of wood.

Painting and Finishing

1. On the clown wood piece, drill a ⁵⁄₁₆" wide hole in the edge between thumb and fingers, catty corner, to come out at the edge of little finger on the top edge. The balloon ribbons will go through the hole when the clock is finished.
2. Stain back side of both the clown and the balloons, and seal both sides of each piece.
3. Paint a coat of white gesso on the top side of each piece.
4. Paint the face and hand flesh-tone. Shadow with medium flesh and highlight with light ivory. Paint area around mouth and upper eyes white. Paint nose and lips red. Paint eyeballs and eye-

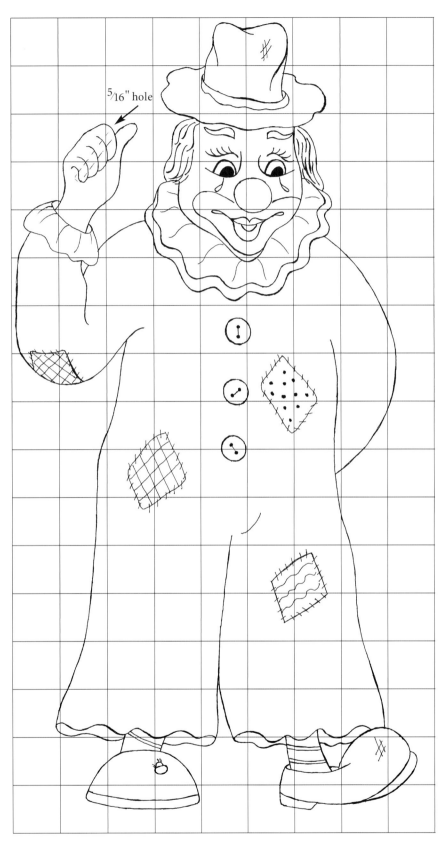

⁵⁄₁₆" hole

Copy pattern at 200%. Finished size of the clown is about 8½" wide by 16½" high.

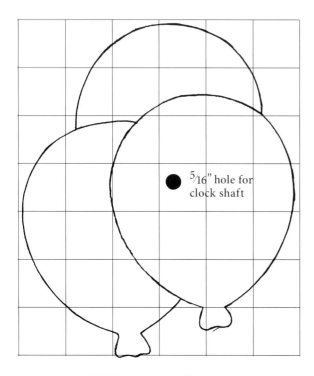

5/16" hole for clock shaft

Copy pattern at 200%. Finished size of the balloons are 6" wide by 7" high.

brows black. Paint spot in mouth black. Paint black teardrop strokes for teardrops and comma strokes at edges of mouth.

5. Paint hair raw sienna. Lighten by mixing with white to highlight hair. Paint hat brown velvet. Paint the band black. Highlight with palomino tan.

6. Paint the suit half Wedgwood blue and half nightfall blue. With the wood end of your brush, put blue mist dots on the Wedgwood. Paint ruffles and socks blue mist. Shadow Wedgwood blue with Cape Cod blue and highlight with blue mist. Shadow nightfall blue with midnight blue and highlight with Wedgwood. Shadow blue mist with Wedgwood and highlight with white.

7. Paint the patches tomato spice (bright red) and the stitching for the patches black. Use black or straw for the lines and dots on the patches. Use Wedgwood to decorate socks. Paint the buttons nightfall blue. Put tiny dots on the button and pull a line between them for thread with Wedgwood blue. Highlight with Wedgwood. Paint the shoes black and highlight with lichen grey.

8. Paint each balloon a different color as follows: tomato spice and highlight with Indiana rose; Cape Cod blue and highlight with Wedgwood blue; and sunbright yellow and highlight with white.

9. Spray with a clear high-gloss acrylic finish.

10. Attach a sawtooth hanger on back of each piece. Assemble clock movement, numbers, and hands on the finished balloons piece.

11. Attach 24" lengths of narrow ribbon to the balloons, and thread them through the hole in the hand.

Puppy Bank

Front of bank. Copy pattern at 225%. Finished size of the puppy: about 9¼" wide by 13½" high (not including the base).

screw   **screw**

Additional supplies:

- Two 1½" flat-head screws
- Two clear 6" × 4½" oval bank sides. The sides should be about ½" larger than the hole in the bank all around
- Gold round-head screws to attach sides

Making the Bank

The puppy part of the bank is one piece of wood with different patterns wood-burned on either side.

1. Trace outline of enlarged front pattern on poster paper, cut out pattern, and trace on 2" pine wood. Trace the base suited for the puppy (given on page 139) on 1" pine wood.

2. Saw out puppy and base and sand well. Drill two ¼" holes through the base where they are marked on the pattern, and make marks for holes on the bottom edge of the puppy for screws. Drill smaller holes in the puppy. With a ½" Forstner bit, drill over the top of the holes on the bottom of the base, approximately ¼" deep, so the screws will be countersunk when finished. With a roundover bit, rout the edge on the top side of base.

3. Trace the detailed patterns onto the front and back of the puppy wood piece, and detail with a wood-burning tool. Sand again with 320-grit sandpaper to remove trace marks, sap, and ashes. Stain and seal both pieces.

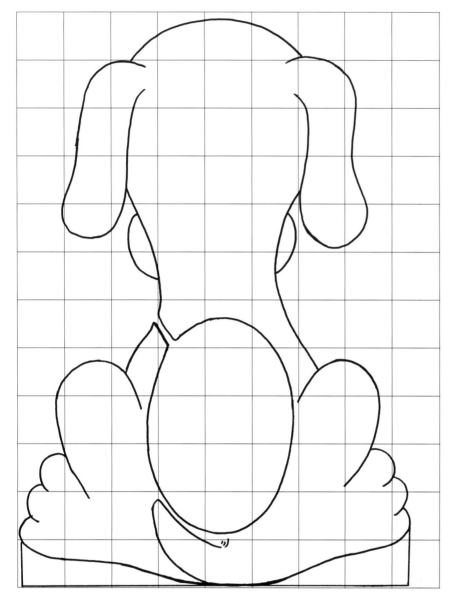

Detailed pattern for back of puppy bank. Copy at 225% for wood-burning.

Painting and Finishing

1. For both sides, shadow with brown velvet and highlight with palomino tan.
2. Paint eyes, nose, and pads on bottom of feet black. Paint black eyelashes. Float adobe on the tongue and highlight with white. Paint white upside-down comma on the left side of the eyes and a small comma on the right side. Paint white upside-down commas on the nose for nostrils.
3. Spray both sides with a clear high-gloss acrylic finish.
4. Attach crystal clear plastic ovals to each side of the puppy, over the hole, with small gold round-head screws.
5. Attach base to puppy with screws.

Walking Kitten Bank

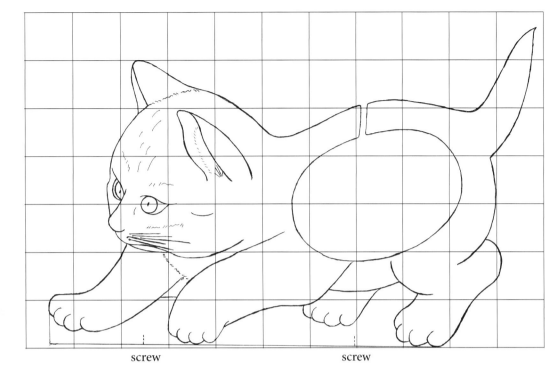

Copy pattern at 265%. Finished size of the kitten is about 13½" wide by 9" high (not including the base).

screw   screw

Additional supplies:

- Two 1½" flat-head screws
- Two clear 6" × 4½" oval bank sides. Sides should be about ½" larger than the hole in the bank all around
- Gold round-head screws to attach sides

Making the Bank

The kitten part of the bank is one piece of wood with the same pattern wood-burned on either side.

1. Trace outline of enlarged pattern on poster paper, cut out pattern, and trace on 2" pine wood. Copy the base suited for the kitten (on page 139) and trace onto 1" pine.
2. Saw out kitten and base, and sand well. Drill two ¼" wide holes through the base, as marked on the pattern, and mark the holes on the bottom of the kitten. Drill smaller holes in the kitten. With a ½" Forstner bit, drill over the top of the holes on the bottom side of the base, approximately ¼" deep, so the screws will be countersunk when finished. With a roundover bit, rout the edge on top side of base.
3. Trace detailed patterns onto the front and back of the kitten wood piece, and detail with a wood-burning tool. Sand again with 320-grit sandpaper to remove trace marks, sap, and ashes.

Painting and Finishing

1. Stain and seal both sides of both pieces. Shadow with brown velvet. Highlight with palomino tan.
2. Paint eyes Cape Cod blue. Shadow with midnight blue and highlight with blue heaven. Paint a midnight blue upside-down teardrop stroke in the center of each eye. Remember to paint both sides of the kitten.
3. Spray with a clear high-gloss acrylic finish.
4. Attach crystal clear plastic ovals to each side, over the hole, with small gold round-head screws. Attach base to kitten with 1½" screws.

Lamb Bank

Front of lamb. Copy pattern at 235%. Finished size: about 10¼" wide by 13¼" high (not including the base).

Additional supplies:

- Two 1½" flat-head screws
- Two clear 6" × 4½" oval bank sides (which you can purchase from a catalog or crafts store).
  The sides should be about ½" larger than the hole in the bank all around
- Gold round-head screws to attach sides

Making the Bank

The lamb part of the bank is one piece of wood with different patterns wood-burned on either side.

1. Trace outline of enlarged front pattern on paper, cut out front pattern, and trace on 2" pine wood. Trace the base for the lamb (given on page 139) onto 1" pine wood.

2. Saw out lamb and base and sand well. Drill two ¼" wide holes through the base, as indicated on the base pattern, and mark them on the bottom of the lamb.

3. Drill smaller holes in the lamb. With a ½" Forstner bit, drill over the top of the holes on the bottom of the base, approximately ¼" deep, so the screws will be countersunk when finished. With a roundover bit, rout the edge on the top side of the base.

4. Trace detailed patterns onto both front and back of the lamb wood piece, and detail with a wood-burning tool. Sand again with 320-grit sandpaper to remove trace marks, sap, and ashes. Stain and seal both pieces.

Detailed pattern for back of
lamb. Copy at 235% for
wood-burning.

Painting and Finishing

1. Stain and seal both sides of both pieces. Remember to paint both sides of the lamb. Shadow with brown velvet. Highlight with palomino tan.

2. Paint eyes, nose, and hooves black. Highlight nose and hooves with lichen grey. Paint white upside-down comma on the left side of the eye and a tiny white comma on the other side. Paint a tiny white upside-down comma on the nose for nostril. Paint black eyelashes. Paint a black comma for brow and at edge of mouth. Paint the space between the body and ear black.

3. Paint the bow Indiana rose. Shadow with gypsy rose and highlight with white. Paint a gold comma on the end of the ribbon and a tiny comma on the knot. Paint the bell gold.

4. Side-load a flat brush with antique white to paint the curls on head, tail, ears, and feet.

5. Spray with a clear high-gloss acrylic finish.

6. Attach a crystal clear plastic oval to each side with small gold round-head screws.

7. Attach base to lamb with 1½" screws.

Teddy Bear Bank

screw   screw

Front pattern. Copy pattern at 220%. Finished size: about 8" wide by 14" high (not including the base).

cut out pattern for the base suited for the teddy bear (given on page 139), and trace on 1" pine wood.

2. Saw out base and teddy bear, and sand well. Drill two ¼" wide holes through the base, as indicated on pattern, and mark them on the bottom of the teddy bear. Drill smaller holes in the teddy bear. With a ½" Forstner bit, drill over the top of the holes on the bottom side of the base, approximately ¼" deep, so the screws will be countersunk when finished. With a roundover bit, rout the edge on the top side of the base.

3. Trace the detailed patterns onto the front and back of the teddy bear wood piece, and detail with a wood-burning tool. Sand again with 320-grit sandpaper to remove trace marks, sap, and ashes.

4. Stain and seal both sides of both pieces.

Additional supplies:

- Two 1½" flat-head screws
- Two clear 6" × 4½" oval bank sides (which you can purchase from a catalog or crafts store).
  The sides should be about ½" larger than the hole in the bank all around
- Gold round-head screws to attach sides

To Make the Bank

1. Trace outline of enlarged teddy bear front pattern on poster paper, cut out pattern, and trace on 2" pine wood. Trace and

Painting and Finishing

1. Shadow front and back of bear with brown velvet and highlight with palomino tan.

2. On the front, with an old frayed brush, daub muzzle and inside of ears with maple sugar. Float adobe underneath eyes on muzzle and on tongue. Highlight with tiny white commas. Pull adobe lines in the ears.

3. Paint eyes and nose black. Paint white upside-down commas on left side of eyes and a small comma on the right side. Paint white upside-down commas on the nose for nostrils. Highlight muzzle around mouth with white. Paint black eyelashes. Paint a small black comma on both sides of the mouth.

4. Paint the space between legs black on front and back.

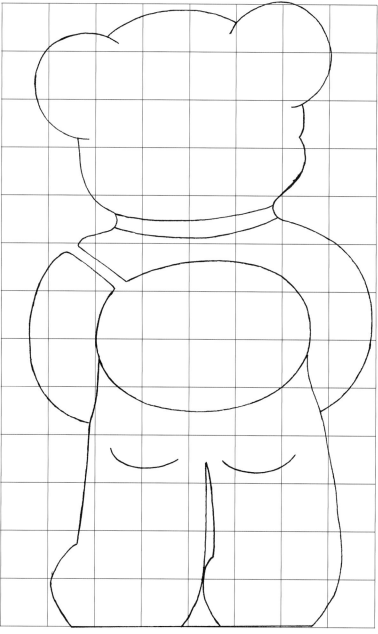

Pattern for back of bank. Copy at 220% for wood-burning.

5. Paint the ribbon and bow tomato spice on front and back. Shadow with maroon and highlight with Indiana rose. Paint a gold comma on each end of the ribbon and gold commas on the knot of the bow.

6. Spray with a clear high-gloss acrylic finish.

7. Attach crystal clear plastic ovals to each side over the hole with small gold round-head screws.

8. Attach base to teddy bear with 1½" screws.

Toy Train Bank

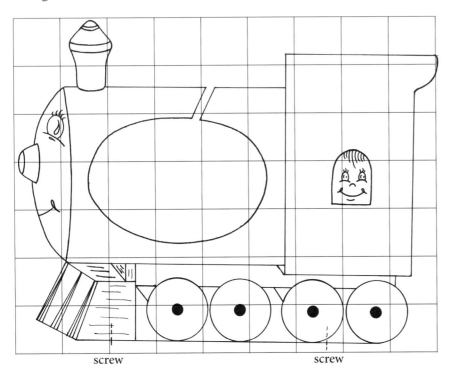

screw   screw

Additional supplies:

- Two 1½" flat-head screws
- Two clear 6" × 4½" oval bank sides (which you can purchase from a catalog or crafts store). The sides should be about ½" larger than the hole in the bank all around
- Gold round-head screws to attach sides

The train part of the bank is one piece of wood with the same pattern on both sides.

1. Trace outline of the enlarged train pattern on poster paper, cut out pattern, and trace on 2" pine wood. Trace the base suited for the toy train (given on page 139) onto 1" pine wood.
2. Saw out train and base and sand well. Drill two ¼" wide holes through the base, as marked on pattern, and mark the holes on the bottom of the toy train. Drill smaller holes in the toy train. With a ½" Forstner bit, drill over the top of the holes on the bottom side of the base, approximately ¼" deep, so the screws will be countersunk when finished. With a roundover bit, rout the edge on the top side of base.
3. Trace the detailed pattern onto both sides of the train piece, and detail with a wood-burning tool. Sand again with 320-grit sandpaper to remove trace marks, sap, and ashes.

Painting and Finishing

1. Stain and seal both base and bank on both sides. Remember to paint both sides of the train. Shadow with brown velvet. Highlight with palomino tan.
2. Paint the eye, ring around nose, rings around smokestack, eyes of face in the window, and wheels black.
3. Use black and white paint for details on train face and face in window (see photo).
4. Paint the nose tip on the train sunbright yellow. Float adobe on the cheek under the eye on the train and on the cheeks of the face in the window.
5. Paint the axles lichen grey. Highlight the wheels with lichen grey.
6. Spray with a clear high-gloss acrylic finish.
7. Attach a crystal clear plastic oval to each side, over the hole, with small gold round-head screws. Attach base to toy train with 1½" screws.

Copy pattern at 255%. Finished size: about 11½" wide by 8¾" high (not including the base).

132

Piggy Bank

Additional supplies:

- Two 1½" flat-head screws
- Two clear 6" × 4½" oval bank sides. The sides should be about ½" larger than the hole in the bank all around
- Gold round-head screws to attach sides

To Make the Bank

The piggy part of the bank is one piece of wood with the same pattern wood-burned into both sides.

1. Trace the outline of the enlarged pig pattern on poster paper, cut out pattern, and trace on 2" pine wood. Trace the base pattern suited for the piggy and copy onto 1" pine wood (given on page 139).
2. Saw out the base and piggy, and sand well. Drill two ¼" wide holes through the base and mark them on the bottom of the piggy. Drill smaller holes in the piggy. With a ½" Forstner bit, drill over the top of the holes on the bottom side of the base, approximately ¼" deep, so the screws will be countersunk when finished. With a roundover bit, rout the edge on the top side of base.
3. Trace detailed piggy pattern onto both sides of the wood piece and detail with a wood-burning tool. Sand again with 320-grit sandpaper to remove trace marks, sap, and ashes.

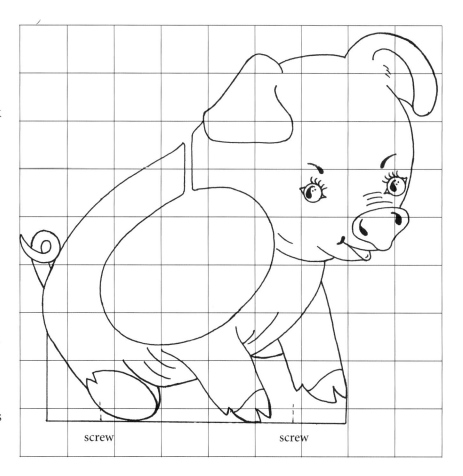

screw   screw

Painting and Finishing

1. Stain and seal both sides of base and pig. Remember to paint both sides of the pig. Shadow with brown velvet. Highlight with palomino tan.
2. Paint eyes, nose, and hooves black. Highlight nose and hooves with lichen grey. Paint a white upside-down comma on one side of the eye and a tiny white comma on the other side. Paint black upside-down commas on the nose for nostrils. Paint black eyelashes. Paint black commas for brows and at edge of mouth. Paint the space in the curl of the tail black. Float adobe on the tongue and highlight with a tiny white comma.

3. Spray with a clear high-gloss acrylic finish.
4. Attach a crystal clear plastic oval to each side, over the hole, with small gold round-head screws. Attach base to piggy with 1½" screws.

Copy pattern at 235%. Finished size: about 10½" wide by 10¼" high (not including the base).

Rocking Horse Clock, Necklace Holder, and Welcome

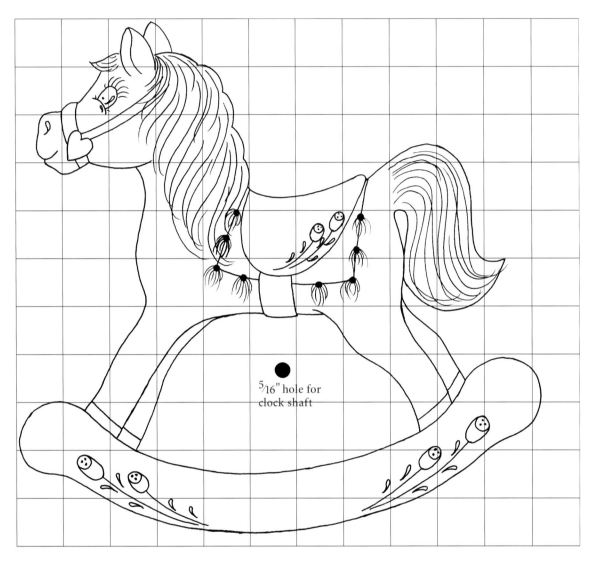

$^5/16$" hole for clock shaft

Clock pattern. Copy at 195%. Finished size of rocking horse is about 11" wide by 10¾" high.

To Start the Clock

1. Copy the enlarged clock pattern, cut out, and prepare wood in the usual way for a clock. Don't cut away the part between the horse's belly and legs and the rocker.
2. Mark and drill a pilot hole where the shaft of the clock will go through. Using a Forstner 3" drill bit, center the tip in the pilot hole on the back side and drill hole approximately ⅜" deep.
3. From the front, center a $^5/16$" drill bit on the pilot hole and drill through for the clock shaft.
4. Paint or stain (see directions on 136 to 137).

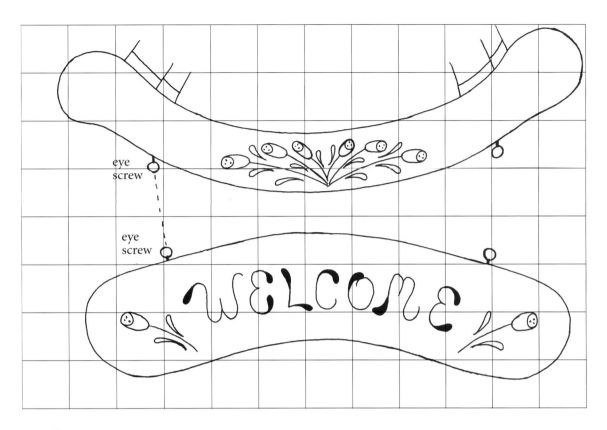

eye
screw

eye
screw

WELCOME

Welcome pattern.
Copy at 195%.

To Start the Necklace Holder

Additional supplies:

• Five 2⅜" long tie pegs

1. Cut out and prepare from the rocking horse clock pattern, but mark and drill five ³⁄₁₆" wide holes, ⅝" deep, in rocker for the tie pegs, spaced as shown on the necklace holder rocker pattern (black dots).
2. Paint or stain the necklace holder (see directions below).

To Start the Welcome

Additional supplies:

• Two 1½" lengths of chain
• Four eye screws

1. Cut out and prepare the rocking horse and the welcome board.
2. Paint or stain the horse and rocker (see directions on pages 136 and 137).

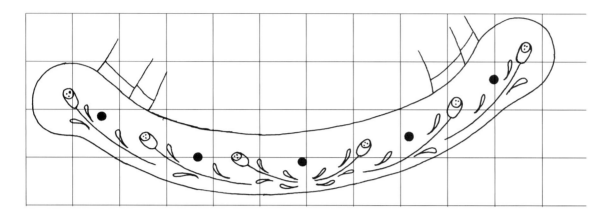

Necklace holder pattern.
Copy at 195%.

For Stained Version (Clock, Necklace Holder, or Welcome)

1. A stained example is the necklace holder shown. Stain and seal both sides of each piece. Shadow horse with brown velvet and highlight with palomino tan.

2. Paint eye, hooves and area between horse and rocker black. Highlight hooves with lichen grey. Dry-brush mane and tail with brown velvet and pull the lines through with burnt umber.

3. Paint a black comma stroke for nostril. Paint a small white upside-down comma stroke on right side of eye and a tiny comma on left side. Paint black eyelashes. Float adobe on cheek and highlight with small white comma stroke.

4. Paint bridle and saddle black. Paint the heart on the bridle and blanket tomato spice.

5. Double-load brush with tomato spice and white for the flowers on both the saddle and rocker.

6. Double-load brush with dark jungle green and Seminole green for the leaves and stems on the rocker.

7. Paint gold commas around flowers. Paint gold commas on heart and around edge of blanket. Put gold dots around edge of saddle and on bridle.

8. Put tomato spice dots around outer edge of blanket and pull lines for fringes. Put tomato spice dots on each end of the rocker.

For Painted Version (Clock, Necklace Holder, or Welcome)

1. See clock for painted example. Stain back side of both pieces and seal both sides of each piece. Apply one coat of gesso on the top sides; then paint the horse sandstone.
2. Shadow with lichen grey and highlight with white. Paint eye, hooves, and area between horse and rocker black. Highlight hooves with lichen grey. Dry-brush mane and tail with lichen grey, and pull the lines through with Quaker grey. Paint a black comma stroke for nostril. Paint a small white upside-down comma on right side of the eye and a tiny comma on the left. Paint black eyelashes. Float adobe on the cheek and highlight with a small white comma stroke.
3. Paint bridle, saddle, and rocker rose mist. Highlight with pink frosting. Paint saddle blanket pink frosting. Shadow with rose mist and highlight with white.
4. Double-load brush with pink frosting and white for the flowers on the saddle and rocker.
5. Double-load brush with dark jungle green and Seminole green for the leaves and stems on rocker.
6. Paint gold commas around flowers. Put rose mist dots around outer edge of saddle and pull lines for fringes. Paint the heart on the bridle gold. Paint tiny gold commas on edge of blanket. Put gold dots on bridle and saddle.

To Finish the Clock

1. After painting or staining, spray with a clear high-gloss acrylic finish.
2. Attach a sawtooth hanger on back. Assemble clock movement, numbers, and hands on the finished piece.

To Finish the Necklace Holder

1. Paint five tie pegs to match horse (for painted version) or stain the tie pegs for the stained version. Put a drop of glue in each hole and insert pegs; then spray with a clear high-gloss acrylic finish.
2. Attach two sawtooth hangers on the back.

To Finish the Welcome

1. Finish the welcome board to match horse (paint for the painted version or stain for the stained version). You may paint "WELCOME" with black and paint flowers on the welcome board. Or use the pre-cut word "WELCOME" and hearts from wood, and paint them to match the horse. You may use the hearts in place of the flowers on the rocker.
2. Glue the "WELCOME" letters and hearts to the welcome board and rocker.
3. Spray with a clear high-gloss acrylic finish.
4. Drill tiny holes on the bottom of the rocker and the top of the welcome (see pattern) for eye screws, and attach chains to eye screws to hang the welcome board from the rocking horse.
5. Attach a sawtooth hanger on the back of the horse.

Rocking Horse Bank

Copy pattern at 235%. Finished size is about 10½" wide by 10⅛" high (not including the base).

screw   screw

Additional supplies:

- Two 1½" flat-head screws
- Two clear 6" × 4½" oval bank sides (which you can purchase from a catalog or crafts store). The sides should be about ½" larger than the hole in the bank all around
- Gold round-head screws to attach sides

The rocking horse part of the bank is one piece of wood with the same pattern wood-burned to decorate both sides.

1. Trace outline of enlarged rocking horse pattern on poster paper, cut out pattern, and trace on 2" pine wood. Copy and trace the base pattern suited for the rocking horse (given on page 139) onto 1" pine wood.
2. Saw out horse and base and sand well. Drill two ¼" wide holes through the base as marked on pattern (circles), and mark on bottom of rocking horse. Drill smaller holes in the rocking horse. With a ½" Forstner bit, drill over the top of the holes on the

bottom of the base, approximately ¼" deep, so the screws will be countersunk when finished. With a roundover bit, rout the edge on the top side of base.

3. Trace the detailed pattern onto both sides of the wood rocking horse piece and detail with a wood-burning tool. Sand again with 320-grit sandpaper to remove trace marks, sap, and ashes.

Painting and Finishing

1. Stain and seal both sides of rocking horse and base. Remember to paint both sides of the horse. Shadow with brown velvet and highlight with palomino tan.
2. Paint eye and hooves black. Highlight hooves with lichen grey. Paint a small white upside-down comma on the one side of the eye and a tiny comma on the other side. Paint black eyelashes.
3. Float adobe on the cheek and highlight with a tiny white comma. Dry-brush mane and tail with brown velvet and pull the lines through with burnt umber. Paint a black comma stroke for nostril.

Base Patterns for Banks

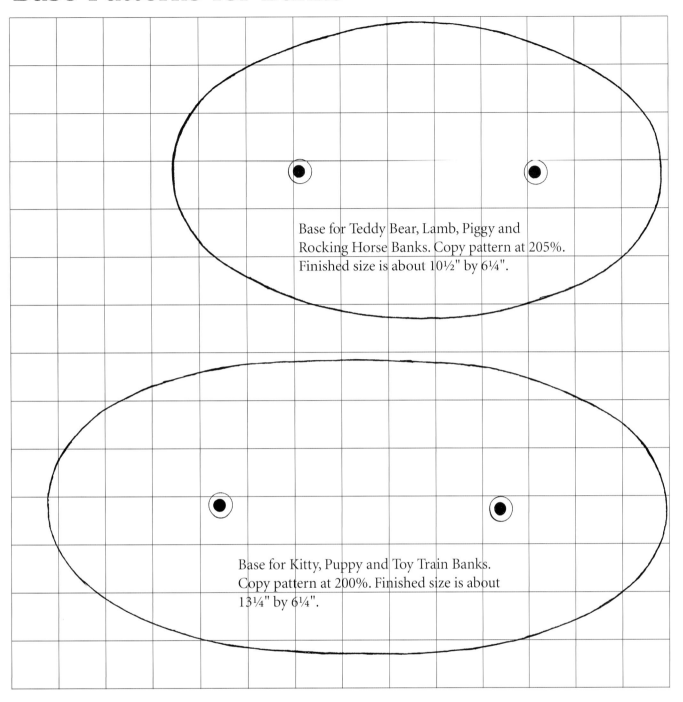

Base for Teddy Bear, Lamb, Piggy and Rocking Horse Banks. Copy pattern at 205%. Finished size is about 10½" by 6¼".

Base for Kitty, Puppy and Toy Train Banks. Copy pattern at 200%. Finished size is about 13¼" by 6¼".

4. Paint bridle and saddle spice tan. Shadow with brown velvet and highlight with maple sugar.

5. Paint the rocker brown velvet. Highlight with palomino tan. Paint the blanket tomato spice. Shadow blanket with maroon and highlight with white.

6. Double-load a flat brush with tomato spice and white for the flowers on the saddle and rocker. Double-load with dark jungle green and Seminole green for the leaves and stems on rocker and saddle.

7. Paint gold commas around flowers. Paint the heart on the bridle gold. Put gold dots on the bridle and around edge of saddle. Put gold dots on each end of the rocker. Put gold dots on the outer edge of the blanket and pull lines for fringes.

8. Spray with a clear high-gloss acrylic finish.

9. Attach crystal a clear plastic oval to each side of the horse, covering the hole, with small gold round-head screws.

10. Attach the base to the rocking horse with 1½" screws.

Mallard Duck Coat Rack

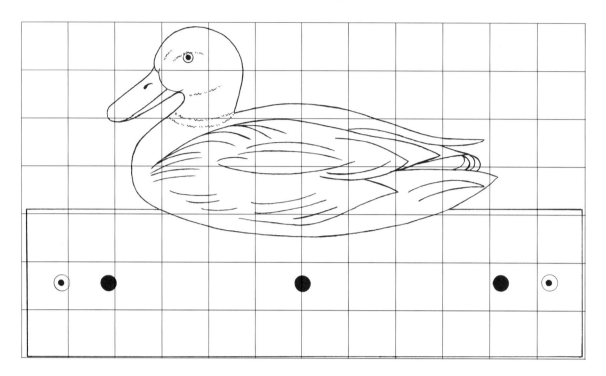

Additional supplies:

- Two 1½" wood screws
- Two ½" screw hole plugs
- Three 3½" Shaker pegs

To Start

1. Trace outline of enlarged pattern on paper, cut out pattern, and trace on ¾" pine wood.
2. Saw out and sand well. Mark and drill three ½" wide holes, ⅝" deep, for the Shaker pegs (black circles on pattern). Mark and drill ³⁄₁₆" wide holes through at each end for wall mounting (white circles on pattern). With a ½" Forstner bit, drill over the top of these two holes, approximately ¼" deep, so the plugs will fit in and cover the screw heads.
3. Trace detailed pattern onto the wood piece and detail with a wood-burning tool. Sand again with 320-grit sandpaper to remove trace marks, sap, and ashes.

Painting and Finishing

1. Stain and seal. Shadow with brown velvet and highlight with palomino tan.
2. Paint eye, ring around neck, and beak straw. Shadow with antique gold and highlight with antique white. Paint a small comma stroke with antique gold on the beak for the nostril. Put a black dot in center of eye.
3. Paint head black green. Shadow with black and highlight with village green or mint green.
4. Paint curled-up tail feathers black.
5. Install 3½" Shaker pegs.
6. Spray with a clear high-gloss acrylic finish. Spray the ½" round-top screw plugs separately.
7. After the coat rack is attached to the wall, cover the screws with the screw hole plugs.

Copy pattern at 295%. Finished size is about 17½" wide by 10¼" high.

Music Staff Calendar Holder

Additional supplies:

- Two 2" carriage bolts with washers and wing nuts
- 3" × 5" notepad or 10⅝" × 8¼" calendar pad

To Start

1. Trace outline of pattern on poster paper, cut out pattern, and trace on ¾" pine wood. Center the calendar holder pattern on the full width of the board. (Since the 1" × 12" lumber varies in width, adjust the width of the holder accordingly.)
2. Saw out and sand well. Saw and sand a wooden bar as long as the width of the holder and ¾" wide, which will hold the calendar pad. Position the bar on the calendar holder, and drill two 5/16" wide holes through both pieces. On the back side of holder, drill a ¾" wide hole, ⅜" deep, with a Forstner bit over top of each 5/16" wide hole, so bolts will be inset.
3. Trace detailed pattern onto the wood piece, and detail with a wood-burning tool. Sand again with 320-grit sandpaper to remove trace marks, sap, and ashes.

Painting and Finishing

1. Stain and seal whole surface.
2. Paint clefs, flats, notes, and dots black. Paint black notes on the bar that holds the calendar pad or paint "HAVE A NICE DAY," with dot flowers on each side of the lettering.
3. Spray with a clear high-gloss acrylic finish.
4. Attach a sawtooth hanger on back. Assemble carriage bolts through the calendar holder, calendar pad, and bar.

The calendar pad may be created in Word, WordPerfect, or any other program that creates calendars. Print on 24 lb. paper. (Lighter weight paper has a tendency to curl.)

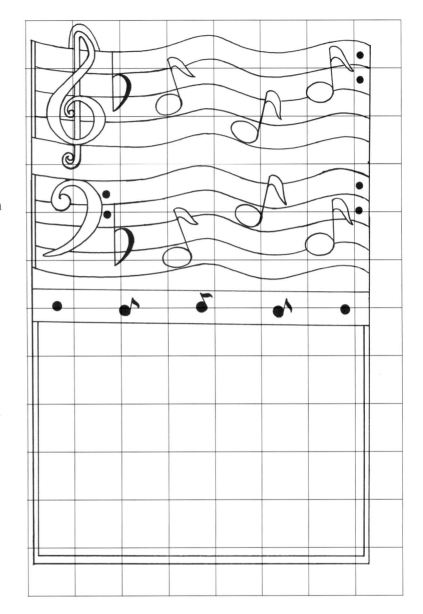

Copy pattern at 305%. Finished size of the calendar holder is about 11" wide × 17" long.

Seated Kitty Calendar or Notepad Holder

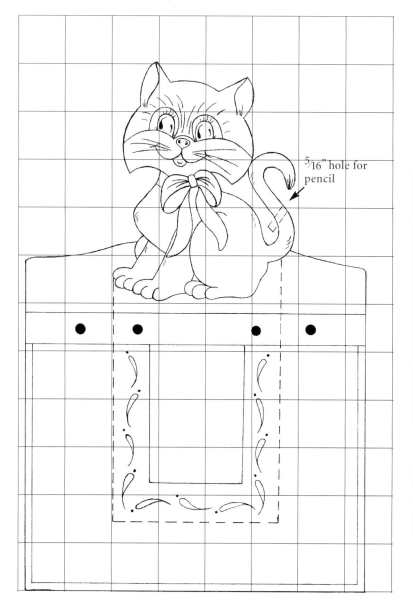

5/16" hole for pencil

Copy pattern at 305%. Finished size of the kitty calendar holder is about 11" wide by 17" high. The notepad holder is about 5⅜" wide by 14½" high.

Additional supplies:

- Two 2" carriage bolts with washers and wing nuts
- 3" × 5" notepad or 10⅝" × 8¼" calendar pad

To Start (Both)

1. Trace outline of enlarged pattern on poster paper, cut out pattern, and trace on ¾" pine wood. The dashed lines on pattern mark the size of the notepad holder.

2. Center the calendar holder pattern using the full width of the board. (Since the 1" × 12" lumber varies in width, adjust the width of the holder accordingly.)

3. Saw out and sand well. Saw and sand a wooden bar that is as long as the width of the holder and ¾" wide, which will hold the calendar pad or notepad in place. Put its length on straight grain.

4. Position the bar on the calendar holder (or notepad holder), and drill two 5/16" wide holes through both pieces at the black dots marked on the pattern. On the back of the holders, drill a ¾" wide hole, ⅜" deep, with a Forstner bit over the top of the 5/16" holes so the bolts will be inset.

5. Drill a 5/16" wide hole in the tail to hold a pencil.

6. Trace detailed pattern onto the wood piece, and detail with a wood-burning tool. Sand again with 320-grit sandpaper to remove trace marks, sap, and ashes.

Painting and Finishing Both

1. Stain and seal whole surface. Shadow with brown velvet. Highlight with palomino tan.

2. Paint eyes, nose, and space between body and tail black. Paint white upside-down comma on the left side of the eyes and a tiny white comma on the other side. Paint tiny upside-down commas on the nose for nostrils. Float adobe on the tongue and highlight with tiny white comma. Paint black eyelashes.

3. Paint the bow heritage blue. Shadow with midnight blue and highlight with Wedgwood blue. Paint a gold comma on each end of the ribbon and a tiny comma on the knot.

For the Calendar Holder

1. Paint "HAVE A NICE DAY" on the bar. Paint flowers on each side to match the bow on the kitty.

2. Spray with a clear high-gloss acrylic finish.

3. Attach a sawtooth hanger on back. Assemble carriage bolts through the calendar holder, calendar pad and bar.

4. The calendar pad may be created in Word, WordPerfect, or any other program that makes calendars. Print on 24 lb. paper. (Lighter weight paper has a tendency to curl.)

For the Notepad Holder

1. Paint "NOTES" on the bar. Paint a border around edge of holder made of Wedgwood blue commas and heritage blue dots, using the wood end of the brush.

2. Spray with a clear high-gloss acrylic finish.

3. Attach a sawtooth hanger on the back. Assemble carriage bolts through the notepad holder and bar.

4. Slip a 3" by 5" notepad between the bar and holder.

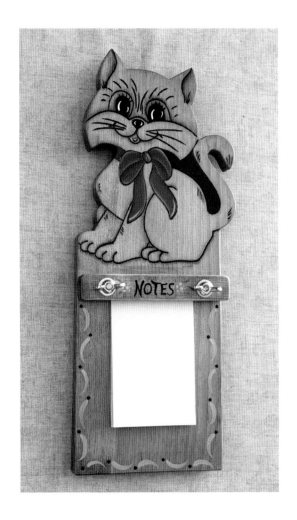

School Pictures Photo Holder

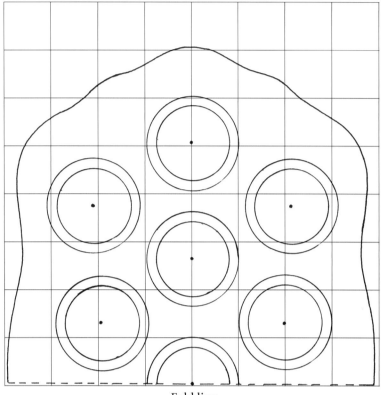

Fold line

Additional supplies needed for this project:

• 39 turn buttons and screws
• 8½" × 11" piece of ¹⁄₁₆" thick clear plastic or acetate (sometimes used for overhead projection)
• Cardboard
• Poster paper, about 10" × 18"
• Ruling compass

Creating, Painting, and Finishing

1. Enlarge pattern and trace outline of half-pattern on poster paper; then turn pattern over and trace the other half on paper for an overall size of 9¾" × 17½". Cut out pattern and trace on ¾" pine wood. Saw out and sand well.
2. Rout the edges of the wood piece. Mark center dots in the circles and drill ¹⁄₁₆" pilot holes. With a 2½" Forstner bit, center the tip into pilot hole, and drill ³⁄₁₆" deep, from the back. From the front, use a 2" Forstner bit; center tip into the pilot hole, and drill through. Rout around the edge of each hole with a roundover bit on the front side.
3. Saw thirteen 2½" diameter circles out of ¹⁄₁₆" crystal clear plastic. If using acetate in place of the ¹⁄₁₆" clear plastic, cut out thirteen 2½" film circles with scissors.
4. Stain and seal wood piece.
5. Paint flowers or some other border around outside edge of the frame, along with the child's name.
6. Spray with a clear high-gloss acrylic finish.
7. Cut out thirteen 2½" diameter cardboard circles.
8. Attach a sawtooth hanger on back to hang the photo holder, and arrange 3 turn buttons around each hole to hold the cardboards on the back. Assemble the clear plastic circles (or film), your pictures, and cardboard circles. Hold in place with the turn buttons.

Note: If the pictures don't fill the circles, cut out 2½" plain white or colored paper circles, and place them between the pictures and the cardboard to form a background.

Copy half-pattern at 245%. Finished size is about 9¾" × 17½".

144

Rocking Horse Coat Rack

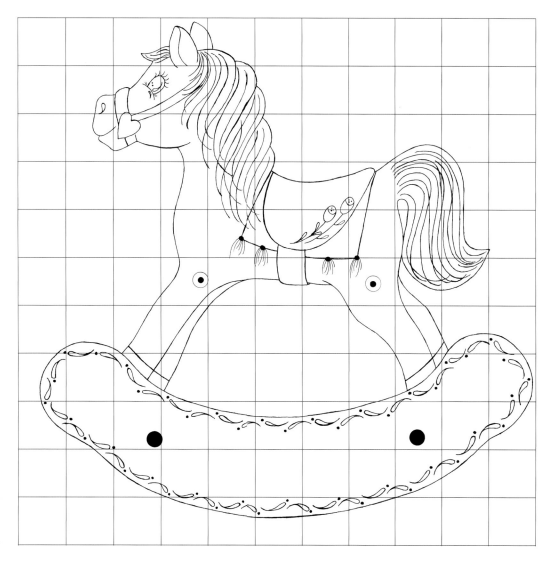

Copy pattern at 310%. Finished size: about 16" wide by 15¾" high.

Additional supplies:

- Two 1½" wood screws
- Two ½" screw hole plugs
- Two 3½" Shaker pegs
- Poster paper, 17" × 17"

To Start

The Rocking Horse Coat Rack pictured is made from ¾" birch plywood, stained with American walnut.

1. Trace outline of pattern on poster paper, cut out pattern, and trace on ¾" birch plywood.
2. Saw out and sand well. (If you make it from birch plywood, sand lightly with 220-grit sandpaper.) Mark and drill two ½" wide holes, ⅝" deep, at the black dots on the pattern for the Shaker pegs. Mark and drill ³⁄₁₆" wide holes through the wood at the

white circles marked on the legs for wall mounting. With a ½" Forstner bit, drill over the top of these two holes, approximately ¼" deep, so the screw hole plugs will fit in and cover the screw heads, but don't install them.

3. Trace detailed pattern onto the wood piece and detail with a wood-burning tool. Sand again with 320-grit sandpaper to remove trace marks, sap, and ashes.

Painting and Finishing

1. Stain and seal both sides. Shadow with brown velvet and highlight with palomino tan.
2. Paint eye, hooves, and area between horse and rocker black. Highlight hooves with lichen grey.
3. Dry-brush mane and tail with brown velvet, and pull the lines through with burnt umber.
4. Paint a black comma stroke for nostril. Paint a small white upside-down comma stroke on right side of eye and a tiny comma on left side. Paint black eyelashes.

5. Float adobe on cheek; highlight with a small white comma stroke. Paint saddle black. Paint the heart on the bridle gold. Paint the bridle and blanket tomato spice.
6. Double-load a brush with tomato spice and white for the flowers on the saddle. Double-load a brush with dark jungle green and Seminole green for the leaves and stems.
7. Paint gold commas around flowers. Paint tiny gold commas around edge of blanket. Put gold dots around edge of saddle and on bridle.
8. Put black dots along the lower edge of blanket and pull lines for fringes. Put tomato spice commas and black dots around the edge of the rocker.
9. Install the 3½" Shaker pegs.
10. Spray with a clear high-gloss acrylic finish. Spray the ½" round-top screw plugs separately.
11. After the coat rack is mounted on the wall with the screws, cover the screw holes with the screw plugs.

Cow Calendar or Notepad Holder

Additional supplies:

• Two 2" carriage bolts with washers and wing nuts
• 3" × 5" notepad or 10⅝" × 8¼" calendar pad

To Start (Both)

1. Trace outline of pattern on poster paper, cut out pattern, and trace on ¾" pine wood. (Dashed line is notepad holder outline.) Center the calendar holder pattern on the wood, using the full width of the board. (Since the 1" × 12" lumber varies in width, adjust the width of the holder accordingly.)

2. Saw out and sand well. Saw and sand a wood bar as long as the width of the holder and ¾" wide, which will hold the calendar pad or notepad in place. The length of bar should be on straight grain of wood.

3. Position the bar on the calendar holder (or notepad holder) and drill two ⁵⁄₁₆" wide holes through both pieces, at the places marked on the pattern by black dots. On the back of the holder, drill a ¾" wide hole, ⅜" deep, with a Forstner bit, over the top of each of the ⁵⁄₁₆" holes, so the bolts will be inset.

4. Drill a ⁵⁄₁₆" wide hole in the shoulder to hold a pencil.

5. Trace the detailed pattern onto the wood piece and detail with a wood-burning tool. Sand again with 320-grit sandpaper to remove trace marks, sap, and ashes.

Painting and Finishing (Both)

1. Stain and seal whole surface. Shadow with brown velvet. Highlight with palomino tan.

2. Paint eyes black. Shadow eyelids with brown velvet. Paint white upside-down commas on the left side of the eyes and a tiny comma on the right side. Paint black eyelashes.

3. Paint black lines at the base of the ear for hair (inside).

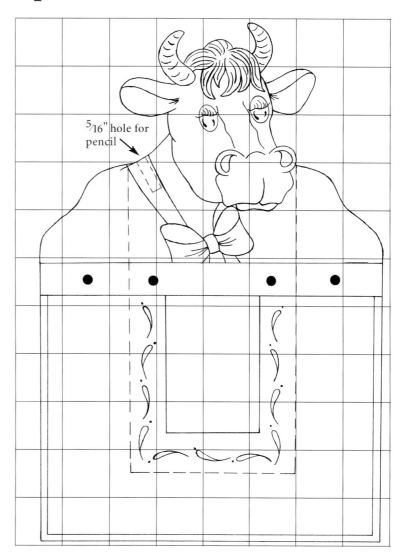

⁵⁄₁₆" hole for pencil

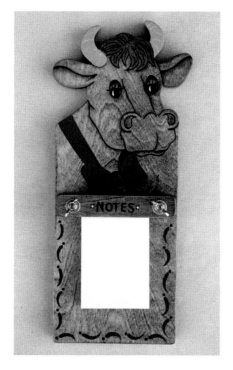

Copy pattern at 305%. Finished size of the cow calendar holder is about 11" wide by 16½" high. The notepad holder is about 5⅜" wide by 14" high.

4. Put a brown velvet wash on the hair on top of the head. Highlight with palomino tan. Shadow inside the nostrils with brown velvet. Paint the horns lichen grey. Paint white lines on the horns using a liner brush. Paint the bow Indiana rose. Shadow with gypsy rose and highlight with white. Paint tiny gold commas on the knot. Then continue as described below.

For the Calendar Holder

1. Paint "HAVE A NICE DAY" on the bar. Paint flowers on each side to match the bow on the cow.
2. Spray with a clear high-gloss acrylic finish.
3. Attach a sawtooth hanger on back. Assemble carriage bolts through the calendar holder, calendar pad and bar.

The calendar pad itself may be created in Word, WordPerfect, or any other program that creates calendars. Print on 24 lb. paper. (Lighter weight paper has a tendency to curl.)

For the Notepad Holder

The notepad holder pictured is made from ¾" birch plywood, stained with American walnut.

1. Paint "NOTES" on the bar. Paint a border around edge of holder of Indiana rose commas and white dots (using the wood end of the brush).
2. Spray with a clear high-gloss acrylic finish.
3. Attach a sawtooth hanger on back. Assemble carriage bolts through the calendar holder, calendar pad, and bar.
4. Slip a 3" by 5" notepad between the bar and holder.

Cow Coat Rack

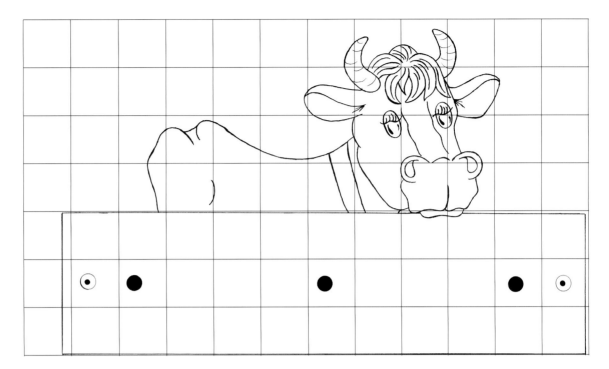

Additional supplies:

- Two 1½" wood screws
- Two ½" screw hole plugs
- Three 3½" Shaker pegs
- Poster paper, 18" × 12"

Making the Rack

1. Trace outline of enlarged pattern on paper, cut out pattern, and trace on ¾" pine wood.

2. Saw out and sand well. Mark and drill three ½" wide holes, ⅝" deep, for the Shaker pegs. Mark and drill a ³⁄₁₆" wide hole through wood at each end (at white circles on pattern) for wall mounting; with a ½" Forstner bit, drill over the top of these two holes approximately ¼" deep so the plugs will fit in and cover the screw heads.

3. Trace the detailed pattern onto the wood piece, and detail with a wood-burning tool. Sand again with 320-grit sandpaper to remove trace marks, sap, and ashes.

Painting and Finishing

1. Stain and seal whole surface.

2. Paint eyes black. Shadow eyelids with brown velvet. Paint white upside-down commas on the left side of the eyes and a tiny comma on the right side. Paint black eyelashes.

3. Paint black lines at the base of the ear for hair inside. Put a brown velvet wash on the hair on top of the head. Highlight with palomino tan. Shadow inside of nostrils with brown velvet. Paint the horns lichen grey. Paint white lines on the horns, using a liner brush. Paint the ribbon Wedgwood blue. Shadow with Cape Cod blue and highlight with blue mist.

4. Install 3½" Shaker pegs. Spray with a clear high-gloss acrylic finish. Spray the ½" round-top screw plugs separately.

5. After the coat rack is mounted on the wall with screws, cover the screw holes with the screw plugs.

Copy pattern at 305%. Finished size: about 17" wide by 10¾" high.

Horse Coat Rack

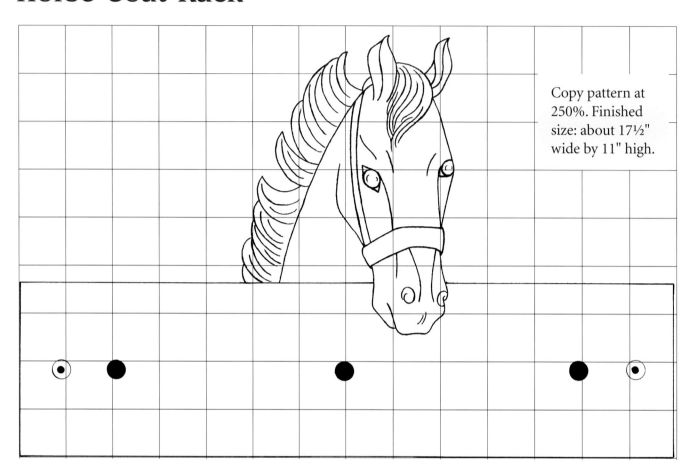

Copy pattern at 250%. Finished size: about 17½" wide by 11" high.

Additional supplies:

- Two 1½" wood screws
- Two ½" screw hole plugs
- Three 3½" Shaker pegs
- Poster paper, 17" × 17"

Making, Painting, and Finishing

1. Trace outline of enlarged pattern on poster paper, cut out pattern, and trace on ¾" pine wood.
2. Saw out and sand well. Mark and drill three ½" wide holes, ⅝" deep, at the black dots on the pattern for the Shaker pegs. Mark and drill ³⁄₁₆" wide holes through the wood at the white circles on the pattern for wall mounting. With a ½" Forstner bit, drill over the top of these two holes about ¼" deep so the screw plugs will fit in and cover the screw heads, but don't install them yet.
3. Trace detailed pattern onto the wood piece, and detail with a wood-burning tool. Sand again with 320-grit sandpaper to remove marks, sap, and ashes.
4. Stain and seal. Shadow with brown velvet and highlight with palomino tan.

5. Paint eyes and mane black. Paint tiny white commas on eyes. Highlight mane with lichen grey. Paint halter candy bar brown. Highlight with Indiana rose. Put gold dots on halter. Install 3½" Shaker pegs.
6. Spray with a clear high-gloss acrylic finish. Spray the ½" round-top screw plugs separately.
7. After the coat rack is mounted on the wall with screws, cover the screw holes with the screw plugs.

Horse Calendar or Notepad Holder

Additional supplies:

- Two 2" carriage bolts with washers and wing nuts
- 3" × 5" notepad or 1⅝" × 8¼" calendar pad

To Start (Both)

1. Trace outline of enlarged pattern on poster paper, cut out pattern, and trace on ¾" pine wood. Dashed line is notepad holder outline. The notepad holder pictured is made from ¾" birch plywood, stained American walnut. Center the calendar holder pattern on the full width of the board. (Since the 1" × 12" lumber varies in width, adjust the width of the holder accordingly.)
2. Saw out and sand well. Saw and sand a wood bar as long as the width of the holder and ¾" wide, which will hold the calendar pad or notepad in place.
3. Position the bar on the calendar holder (or notepad holder) and drill two ⁵⁄₁₆" wide holes through both pieces at the places marked on the pattern by black dots. On the back of the holders, drill a ¾" wide hole, ⅜" deep, with a Forstner bit over top of each of the ⁵⁄₁₆" holes, so the bolts will be inset.
4. Drill a ⁵⁄₁₆" wide hole in the mane to hold a pencil.
5. Trace the detailed pattern onto the wood piece, and detail with a wood-burning tool. Sand again with 320-grit sandpaper to remove trace marks, sap, and ashes.

Copy pattern at 300%. Finished size of the calendar holder: about 11" wide by 17¾" high. Finished size of notepad holder: about 5⅜" wide by 15" high.

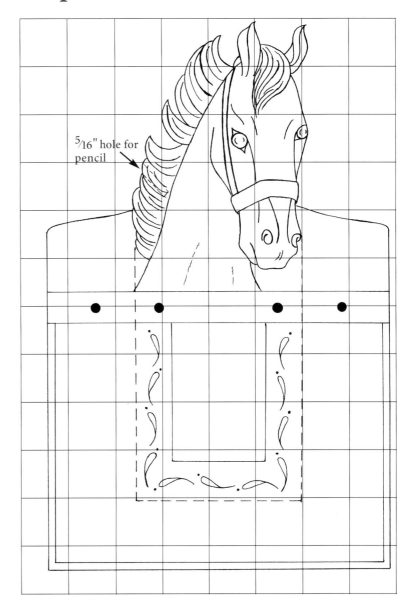

⁵⁄₁₆" hole for pencil

Painting (Both)

1. Stain and seal whole surface. Shadow with brown velvet. Highlight with palomino tan.
2. Paint eyes and mane black. Highlight the mane with lichen grey. Paint tiny white commas on the eyes.
3. Paint the halter candy bar brown. Highlight with Indiana rose. Put gold dots on the halter. Then continue as described below.

For the Calendar Holder

1. Paint "HAVE A NICE DAY" on the bar. Paint flowers on each side to match the horse's halter.
2. Spray with a clear high-gloss acrylic finish.
3. Attach a sawtooth hanger on back. Assemble carriage bolts through the calendar holder, calendar pad, and bar.

The calendar pad may be created in Word, WordPerfect, or any other program that makes calendars. Print on 24 lb. paper. (Lighter weight paper has a tendency to curl.)

For the Notepad Holder

1. Paint "NOTES" on the bar. Paint a border around edge of holder of candy bar brown commas and black dots, using the wood end of the brush.
2. Spray with a clear high-gloss acrylic finish.
3. Slip a 3" by 5" notepad between the bar and holder.

152

Mallard Duck Welcome

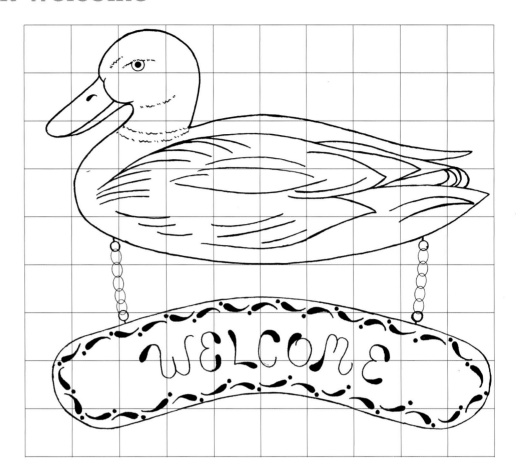

Copy pattern at 225%. Finished size of duck with welcome sign attached: about 10½" wide by 9¼" high.

Additional supplies:

- Two 1" to 2" lengths of chain
- 4 eye screws

To Start

1. Trace outline of each pattern (duck and welcome sign board) on poster paper, cut out pattern, and trace on ¾" pine wood. Saw out and sand well.
2. Trace detailed pattern onto the duck wood piece, and detail with a wood-burning tool. Sand again with 320-grit sandpaper to remove trace marks, sap, and ashes.

Painting and Finishing

1. Stain and seal whole surface of both pieces. Shadow with brown velvet and highlight with palomino tan.
2. Paint eye, ring around neck, and beak straw. Shadow with antique gold and highlight with antique white. Paint a small comma stroke with antique gold on the beak for the nostril. Put a black dot in center of eye.

3. Paint head black green. Shadow with black and highlight with village green or mint green. Paint curled-up tail feathers black.
4. Daub the sign board with antique white. Paint "WELCOME" on the sign board with black. Paint antique white commas and brown velvet dots around edge.
5. Spray with a clear high-gloss acrylic finish.
6. Attach a sawtooth hanger on back. Assemble using four eye screws and chains to connect the sign to the duck.

Fish #1 Coat Rack

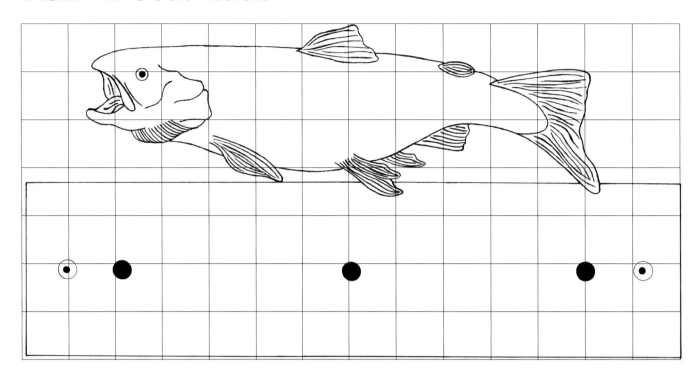

Additional supplies:

- Two 1½" wood screws
- Two ½" screw hole plugs
- Three 3½" Shaker pegs
- Poster paper, 20" × 10"

To Start

1. Trace outline of enlarged pattern on poster paper, cut out pattern, and trace on ¾" pine wood.
2. Saw out and sand well. Mark and drill three ½" wide holes, ⅝" deep, at the black dots on the pattern for the Shaker pegs. Mark and drill ⁵⁄₁₆" wide holes through the wood at the white circles marked on the pattern at each end for wall mounting. With a ½" Forstner bit, drill over the top of these two holes, approximately ¼" deep, so the plugs will fit in and cover the screw heads, but don't install plugs yet.
3. Trace detailed pattern onto the wood piece and detail with a wood-burning tool. Sand again with 320-grit sandpaper to remove trace marks, sap, and ashes.

Painting and Finishing

1. Stain and seal.
2. Highlight with silver. Paint the eye straw and put a

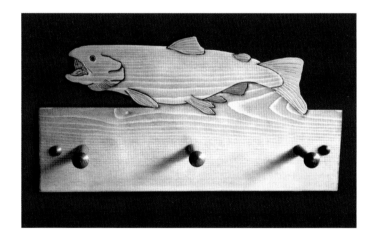

black dot in center with a small amount of straw showing around edge.
3. Triple-load brush with coral, blue spruce, and silver to paint the fins. Put a coral wash on the tongue.
4. Install 3½" Shaker pegs.
5. Spray with a clear high-gloss acrylic finish. Spray the ½" round-top screw plugs separately.
6. After the coat rack is mounted on the wall with screws, cover the screw holes with the screw plugs.

Copy pattern at 250%. Finished size: about 17½" wide by 8¾" high.

Template

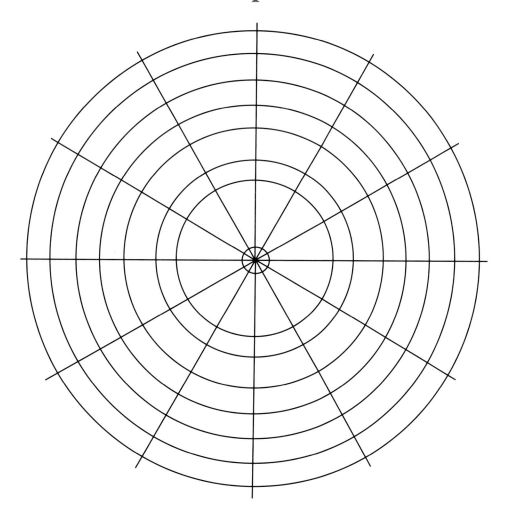

Template for positioning clock numerals. Enlarge as needed.
position numeral on intersection of spoke and circle.

Clock Hands

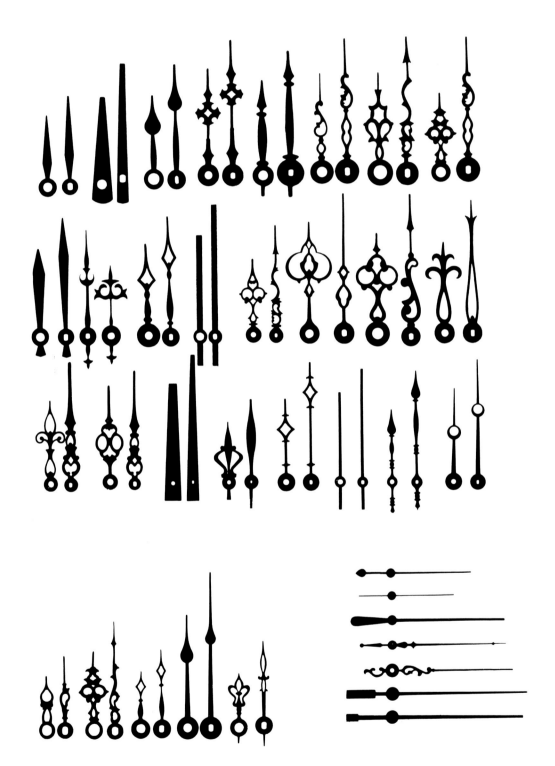

Clock hands. Sweep second hands, lower right.

Metric Equivalents Chart

(to the nearest mm or 0.1 cm)

inches	mm	cm	inches	cm
⅛	3	0.3	20	50.8
¼	6	0.6	21	53.3
⅜	10	1.0	22	55.9
½	13	1.3	23	58.4
⅝	16	1.6	24	61.0
¾	19	1.9	25	63.5
⅞	22	2.2	26	66.0
1	25	2.5	27	68.6
1¼		3.2	28	71.1
1½		3.8	29	73.7
1¾		4.4	30	76.2
2		5.1	31	78.7
2½		6.4	32	81.3
3		7.6	33	83.8
3½		8.9	34	86.4
4		10.2	35	88.9
4½		11.4	36	91.4
5		12.7	37	94.0
6		15.2	38	96.5
7		17.8	39	99.1
8		20.3	40	101.6
9		22.9	41	104.1
10		25.4	42	106.7
11		27.9	43	109.2
12		30.5	44	111.8
13		33.0	45	114.3
14		35.6	46	116.8
15		38.1	47	119.4
16		40.6	48	121.9
17		43.2	49	124.5
18		45.7	50	127.0
19		48.3		

Enlargements of Grid Boxes

1/2" x 195% = .975"

1/2" x 200% = 1"

1/2" x205% = 1.02"

1/2" x 210% = 1.05"

1/2" x 220% = 1.10"

1/2" x 225% = 1.125"

1/2" x 230% = 1.15"

1/2" x 240% = 1.2"

1/2" x 250% = 1.25"

1/2" x 260% = 1.3"

1/2" x 265% = 1.32"

1/2" x 270% = 1.35"

1/2" x 275% = 1.375"

1/2" x 280% = 1.4"

1/2" x 290% = 1.45"

1/2" x 300% = 1.5"

1/2" x 310% = 1.55"

1/2" x 320% =1.6"

1/2" x 330% = 1.65"

1/2" x 350% = 1.75"

1/2" x 375% = 1.875"

Conversion Factors

1 inch=2.54 cm=25.4 mm

1 foot=30.5 cm=304.8 mm

About the Author

I grew up on a farm in central Nebraska. I loved the outdoors and thoroughly enjoyed being with my dad as he did his daily work with the animals, grooming the fields, planting and harvesting the crops. Along with this, there was a lot of fixing and repairing of fences, buildings, and machinery. I found the shop with the wood tools most fascinating. Seems as though my dad was always looking for his tools. Later in life, I began designing and building wooden clocks.

Although I've enjoyed water skiing and snow skiing, bowling was and still is one of my favorite sports. I love horses and my little Yorkie dog.

After retiring from my regular job, I sold my home and relocated to be near my daughter and her family. I am now working for my daughter in her financial consulting office. I am also an active member in my church.

Index